A LINGUISTIC
MAP
OF
SCOTLAND
ca1600 AD

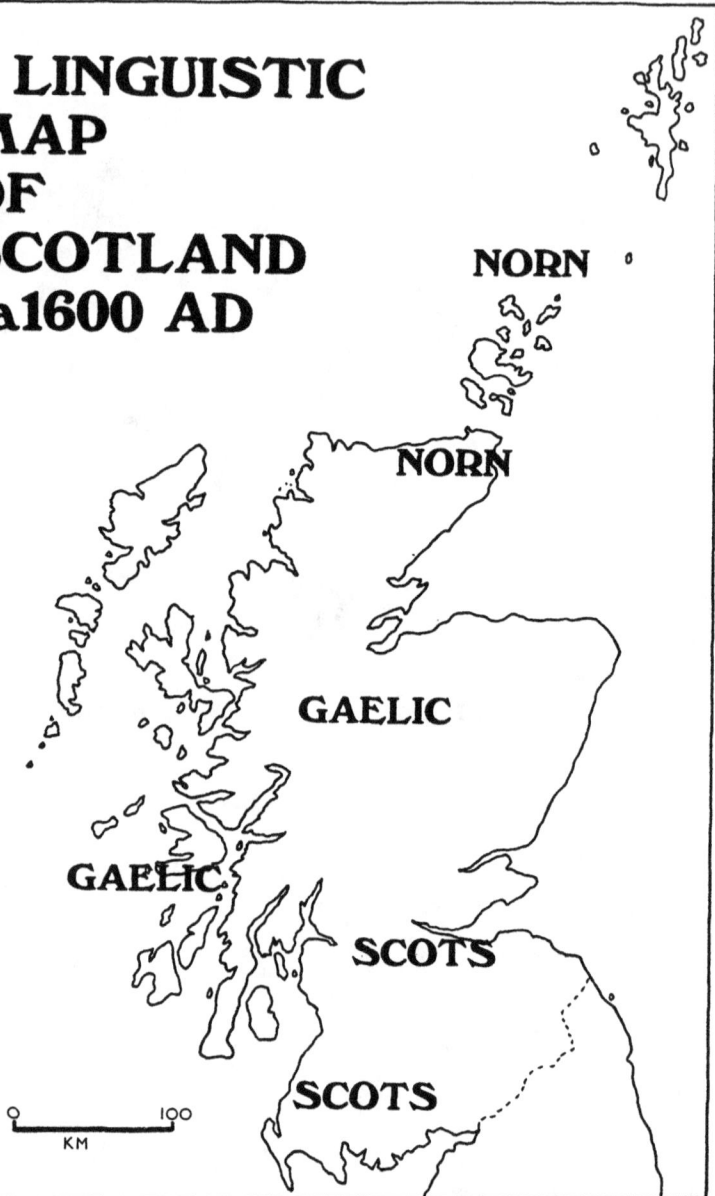

NORN

NORN

GAELIC

GAELIC

SCOTS

SCOTS

0   100
KM

THE
SCOTTISH SURNAMES
OF
COLONIAL
AMERICA

by
David Dobson

CLEARFIELD

Printed for
Clearfield Company, Inc. by
Genealogical Publishing Co., Inc.
Baltimore, Maryland
2003

International Standard Book Number: 0-8063-5209-4

Made in the United States of America

The Scottish Surnames of Colonial America.

INTRODUCTION

Almost all of us have inherited at birth a surname which has descended in the family since medieval times. Few, apart from genealogists who use it as a research tool, give it more than a passing thought. The study of surnames should be more than peripheral to family historians as it provides some insight into the life of an early ancestor and the progenitor of the family.

In Scotland, the use of surnames seems to have begun in the 12th century in the wake of Norman-French immigration. In practice it took many generations for the adoption of the use of surnames by every level of society. Scottish surnames can be categorized into four distinct groups: names of territorial origin, names of occupational origin names of patronymic origin, and names of descriptive origin. Making the situation more complex is the fact that in the beginning there were four distinct linguistic groups: the Picts of the north-east, the Scots of Dalriada based roughly in Argyll, the Britons of the Strathclyde area, and the Angles of Bernicia, from the river Forth to the river Tyne. In addition, there is the small but influential Norse in the far northern areas of Orkney, Shetland and Caithness, together with a smattering of Norman-French and Fleming knights, craftsmen and merchants. By the 12th century the urban dwellers tended to speak a form of English, while rural inhabitants generally spoke Gaelic.

The first people to adopt surnames were the land-owning nobility who required some method of identification and generally took the name of their property as their surnames. For example, the surname Abernethy derives from a place of that name in Strathearn and was first used in 1160 AD by Hugh, the lay abbot of the Culdee monastery there. The majority of early surnames based on indigenous placenames are of Celtic origin (Gaelic, Pictish or British), whereas some from the south-east are of English origin, and some from the Northern Isles are Norse. If a property changed hands, the new owner adopted the name. One of the most famous Scots-Americans was Andrew Carnegie, whose surname comes from a place in Angus. In 1340 John de Ballinard bought the barony of Carnegie and adopted the placename as his surname, becoming John de Carnegie and the progenitor of the Carnegies

Many Scots surnames are derived from placenames owned by an early forebear, such as Pinkerton (i.e. Allan Pinkerton, the detective) or Dallas or Swanston, whereas others identify where the individual came from, examples being Murray, Ross and Sutherland. Those surnames bearing the prefix "Auch", such as Auchmuty, Achinleck or Auchterlonie, are from the Gaelic "achadh," meaning a field; Kilpatrick or Kilgour are from "cil"—a church; Dunbar, Dunlop or Dundas are from "dun"—a fort; and Balfour, Balmaine, Ballantyne or Ballingall are from "bal"—a village.

The Picts, a Celtic people, were absorbed by the Scots in the 9th century, and little trace of their language exists apart from a few placenames, some of which have become surnames. Names with the prefix "pit" meaning 'a share of land,' such as Pitcairn or Pattullo, are from the Pictish language.

From south-east Scotland, formerly Bernicia, the northern province of the Anglian kingdom of Northumbria, come surnames based on English placenames. Names which bear the suffixes of "ham," "ford," "ton" or "wick," (as in Cunningham, Rutherford, Crawford, Renton, Carrington, Borthwick and Fenwick) bear testament to their Anglian origins.

The British or Cymric surnames in Scotland are identified by the prefix "aber" meaning rivermouth, as in Abercromby or Arbuthnott, and "car" meaning a fort, as in Carmichael, Cramond or Carruthers.

A handful of surnames such as Houston (Hugh's town) or Symington (Simon's town) are based on Flemish settlements in 12th century Clydesdale. Norman-French families settling in Scotland brought surnames of continental place names such as Somerville, Gifford, Sinclair or Bethune. Norse placenames in Orkney and Shetland are less common and include Fea, Halcro, Setter, Skea and Twatt.

A substantial number of Scottish surnames come directly from the occupation of an early ancestor. In order to identify individuals with a common Christian name, the title of his occupation was added. In written form these generally appeared in Latin, although in everyday speech they would be in the vernacular. In due course Latin was abandoned in favour of English, and descriptive surnames such as miller, cook, tailor and smith appear. When towns grew, and specialised trades developed, names such as Webster (weaver), Walker (fuller), Litster (dyer), Soutar (shoemaker), Baxter (baker), Fletcher (arrowmaker), Dempster (judge), and many more, appeared.

There being few towns, where tradesmen existed, in the Gaelic speaking areas, few occupational names exist. Exceptions were Gow ("gobha"—smith), Caird ("caerd"—craftsman), and Clachar ("clachair"—stonemason). Some surnames bearing the prefix "Mac" contain an occupational element, e.g. MacSporran (son of the purse bearer) and MacNab (son of the abbot). A few Gaelic surnames bear the prefix "gil" ("gille"—servant) and can be classified as being of occupational origin. Gillespie means servant of the bishop.

Many Scottish surnames are based on patronymics—the system whereby a son would adopt his father's Christian name as his surname, with or without a prefix or suffix. In medieval Scotland the practice was to do this literally, which meant that the surname changed with each generation. This practice was soon, however, abandoned in the lowlands in favour of a fixed and permanent name. In some parts of the Highlands the practice continued until the early 18th century, and in Orkney and Shetland it only died out in the early 19th century. The mainly Norse origin of the inhabitants of these islands maintained the Scandinavian practice of not only adding "son" to a father's forename but also added "dochter" in the case of a daughter. Malcolm Ronaldson, who died in Orkney c.1612 mentioned in his will his wife Janet Malcolmsdochter (her father would have been christened Malcolm) and his sons James, Malcolm and Alexander Malcolmson. However, the vast majority of Scottish patronymics either bear the Gaelic prefix "Mac" or the equivalent English suffix of "son," such as MacDonald, McKay, McAlastair, Robertson, Davidson, Anderson, Thomson, etc.

A number of surnames may originally have been nicknames which identified some feature of an individual's physique or personality. One of the best known and earliest examples of this would be the 11th century King Malcolm III, known as "Canmore" from the Gaelic "ceann mhor" meaning "big head." Some of these names are based on hair colouring or complexion and appear in both English and Gaelic versions; Reid or Roy (Gaelic—"ruadh"—red); White or Bain (Gaelic "ban"—fair); Black or Down (Gaelic "dhu"—black); or Fair or Bowie (Gaelic: "buidhe"—yellow). Some refer to parts of the body such as Armstrong, Cruikshanks or Campbell (Gaelic—"caimbeul"—crooked mouth). Others refer to age, Young or Ogg (Gaelic—"og"—young); Old or Auld or Gemmell (Norse "gemle"—old). Others refer to physique such as Stout, Little, Thinn or Lang. A few are based on racial origins: French, Scott, Inglis, Fleming, Dutch, Welsh (English meaning "foreigner").

Americans researching their Scottish surnames should keep in mind the fact that many names, especially the unusual ones or those of Gaelic origin, have become garbled versions of their original forms. The Anglicised Gaelic name McCorqudale comes from the Gaelic "MacTorquil" which itself is based on a Norse name meaning "Thor's kettle." Similarly names should not be taken at their face value – McTurk does not indicate a Middle Eastern immigrant to Scotland, while McCrone does not mean son of the hag, nor does McQuaker indicate a Scottish member of the Society of Friends. Some surnames which no longer exist in Scotland can be found in America, and others, like McVanish, have simply disappeared!

By 1776 perhaps as many as 150,000 Scots had settled in the American colonies stretching from Hudson Bay to Barbados and brought with them many distinctive surnames. An even greater number of immigrants arrived in the colonies from Ireland, of which a significant portion came from Ulster. Many of those from that province were of Scottish origin and bore Scots surnames. Thus by the late 18th century Scottish surnames were well established in the American colonies. This book attempts to identify these surnames, provide explanations to their meaning and significance, give examples, and where applicable name the clan to which the family is linked.

David Dobson
St Andrews, Scotland, 2003.

THE SCOTTISH SURNAMES OF
COLONIAL AMERICA

ABBOT. A surname of occupational origin, derived from the office of
abbot. Examples in Scotland date from the thirteenth century. The
Gaelic surname '*MacNab*' means son of the abbot. Frederick
Abbot, a Jacobite captured after the Siege of Preston, was
transported to Jamaica or Virginia in 1716. Clan McNab.

ABERCROMBY. A British surname of territorial origin, signifying a
place at the mouth of the Crombie river in Fife. It has existed as a
surname since the thirteenth century. Robert Abercrombie
emigrated to Philadelphia in 1775.

ABERNETHY. A British surname of territorial origin, signifying a place
at the mouth of the Nethy stream. There are two or three places
called Abernethy in Scotland. The earliest example of the surname
dates from the middle of the twefth century with Hugh Abernethy
the lay abbot of the Culdee Monastery in Strathearn. Janet
Abernethy, from Aberdeenshire, was transported to Virginia in
1772.

ADAIR. Possibly a variation of Edgar. Most of the early examples come
from Galloway and date from the fourteenth century. Patrick Adair
and his family, from Wigtownshire, emigrated to New York in 1774.

ADAM. A surname of biblical origin which appeared initially as a
forename. Examples of the name in Scotland can be traced back to
the twefth century. From this surname are derived surnames such as
Adamson, Adie, Eddy, Addison and MacAdam. Among the Scots
transported by Cromwell to New England in 1650 was a James
Adam, while William Adamson, a Covenanter, was banished to
Virginia in 1668, and Francis Adams emigrated from Larne to
Charleston in 1773. Some Adams are connected with the Clan
Gordon.

AGNEW. Territorial, derived from the barony of Agneaux in Normandy
brought to Scotland in the twefth century. The family traditionally
was associated with Galloway in south-west Scotland from where
some of them moved to Ireland in the seventeenth century. Andrew
Agnew settled in Maryland in 1674, Niven Agnew was transported

to Boston in 1650, and John Agnew emigrated from Larne to
Charleston in 1773.

AIKENHEAD. Territorial, derived from the lands of Aikenhead in
Lanarkshire. Examples date from the late thirteenth century such as
Gilbert de l'Akenhead in 1296. William Aitkenhead died in Jamaica
by 1768.

AIKMAN. Descriptive, probably from Old English meaning 'oak-man'.
The first recording of the name in Scotland is of Alexander Akeman
in Lanarkshire during 1296. William Aickman, an Edinburgh
advocate, owned land in East New Jersey in 1684.

AINSLIE. Territorial, derived from a place in England. Examples date
from the early thirteenth century in southern Scotland. Thomas
Ainsley, from Jedburgh, emigrated to Maryland in 1720.

AIR. Territorial, derived from the town of Ayr formerly Air. Also appears
as Ayre, Ayr, and Eyre. Perhaps from Old Norse '*eyri*' meaning
'tongue of land'. The earliest example comes from Berwickshire in
the thirteenth century. William Ayre, a Jacobite, was transported to
Maryland in 1716.

AIRD. Descriptive of a place, probably from Gaelic '*aird*' signifying
'height', Used as a surname since the sixteenth century. James Aird
settled near Pensacola, West Florida, before 1777.

AITCHISON, ACHESON. Patronymics, derived from diminutives of
'*Adam*'. Surnames in Scotland since the fifteenth century, and in
Ulster since the Plantation. John Aitchison, a merchant, died in New
London, Connecticut, in 1770, while John Atcheson settled in New
York during 1775.

AITKEN, AIKEN. Patronymic, a variant of the English name '*Atkin*'
meaning 'little – Adam'. A surname in use in Scotland since the
fifteenth century. Robert Aitken settled in Philadelphia as a
publisher and bookseller in 1769.

ALDCORN. Territorial, derived from a place in Sussex, England.
Recorded in Scotland since the fifteenth century. Reverend Adam
Aldcorn, a Covenanter, was transported to the West Indies in 1678,
and Alexander Alcorn was in New York by 1701.

ALEXANDER. Originally a Greek name. Introduced into Scotland in the
tenth century as a forename and subsequently became a surname. In
Gaelic it appears as Alasdair, Alastair, MacAllister and
MacAlexander. Sir William Alexander of Menstrie, later Earl of

Stirling, was the founder of Nova Scotia in the 1620s. John
Alexander a, a merchant from Edinburgh, died in Carolina in 1699,
and Robert Alexander, an Irish indentured servant, settled in
Philadelphia by 1785. Some Alexanders are septs or the Clan
Donald and others of the McArthurs.

ALISON, ELLISON. Patronymic with an unclear origin possibly
meaning *'son of Alister'* or *'son of Elias'* or *'son of Allan'*. Used in
Scotland since the thirteenth century. Robert Allison was in New
York by 1701, and Patrick Alison was deported to Carolina in 1684.
Clan Donald.

ALLAN. This has dual origins. The first is from the Gaelic *'ailin'*
meaning 'rock', and the second is from Alan, a Breton, who
accompanied William the Conqueror to England in 1066, and within
a century it was recorded in Scotland. Also appears as Alan, Allen,
Callan and MacAllan. Adam Allan, a Covenanter, was banished to
Carolina in 1684. Certain Allans are linked with the McDonalds and
others with the MacFarlanes.

ALLARDYCE. From the old barony of Allardice in Kincardineshire. It
has been used as a surname from the thirteenth century. John
Allardyce was a member of the Scots Charitable Society of Boston
in 1684.

ANCRUM. Derived from the lands of that name near Jedburgh. Possibly
meaning 'at the bend of the (river) Alne'. Used as a surname since
the thirteenth century, with most early examples found in south-east
Scotland. John Ancrum died in Wilmington, North Carolina, in
1779.

ANDERSON. One of the most common Scottish surnames. A corruption
of 'Andrew-son'. St Andrew being the Patron Saint of Scotland
many boys were named Andrew after him leading in due course to
the surname Anderson. In Gaelic it appears as 'MacAindreis' often
Anglicised as MacAndrew. Reverend Charles Anderson was the
minister of Westover parish, Virginia, 1700-1718, while William
MacAndrew was transported to Boston in 1652, and William
Anderson, from Portlanone, Ireland, settled in Pennsylvania by
1769. Some Andersons claim allegiance to the Clan Donald and
others to the Clan Ross.

ANDREW. Based on the Greek name 'Aindrea'. A favourite name in
Scotland as it is the name of the country's patron saint. It appears

both as a forename and a surname. David Andrew, a thief, was transported from Ayr to Barbados in 1653, while William Andrews was a minister in the Mohawk Valley from 1700 to 1728, and James Andrew emigrated from Belfast to Philadelphia in 1773. Andrew is a sept of Clan Ross.

ANGUS. A Gaelic name *'Aonghas'* which dates back to the eighth century. It may also derive from Angus in eastern Scotland. .Robert Angus, a skipper from Fife, sailed to Nova Scotia around 1624, and John Angus from Forfar, Angus, emigrated to New York in 1775. Certain Angus families are septs of the Clan McInnes.

ANNAN. From Annan in Dumfries-shire. Alexander Annan, a Jacobite from Aberdeen was transported to the Chesapeake in 1747 and Walter Annand was banished to East New Jersey in 1685.

ARBUCKLE. Possibly derived from the Gaelic *'ard an buchaille'* the height of the shepherd. Probably from Arbuckle in Lanarkshire. Sixteenth century examples appear as *Arnbukle* or *Arbukill*. John Arbuckle, a Covenanter, was transported to Barbados in 1685, while William Arbuckle, a Glasgow merchant, was admitted to the Scots Charitable Society of Boston in 1684.

ARBUTHNOTT. A territorial name based on a barony in Kincardineshire. From 'Aber-lethnott' the place at the mouth of the Lethnott stream. Thomas Arbuthnott, a surgeon, died in Virginia in 1742, and James Arbuthnott, a minister, was sent to the Leeward Islands in 1705.

ARCHIBALD. An Old English name which has been used as a surname in Scotland since the twefth century. James Archibald sailed from Dunbarton to Nova Scotia in 1627, and John Archibald was a Cromwellian transportee in Boston in 1650.

ARMOUR. Occupational, derived from the occupation of armour-maker. Examples date from the thirteenth century. James Armour, a merchant from Glasgow, settled in Perth Amboy, East New Jersey, in 1687, and John Armour from County Down settled in Virginia by 1750.

ARMSTRONG. Descriptive, this was a common surname among the Border reivers, especially in Liddesdale and the Debateable Land. Some Armstrongs fled to County Fermanagh in the early seventeenth century and today it is one of the most common surnames there. Emigrants included Robert Armstrong from Jedburgh who was banished to Barbados in 1665, Thomas Armstrong from Dumfries to Prince Edward Island in 1775, and Eleanor Armstrong, from Armagh, who emigrated to Philadelphia in 1771. Clan Armstrong.

ARNOT. Used as a surname since the twefth century it originates in the lands of Arnot in Kinross-shire. John Arnot, a Covenanter from Kinross, was transported to the West Indies in 1678, while David Arnott, a Jacobite, was banished to Virginia in 1746.

ARTHUR. Probably from the Gaelic '*Artair*', also MacArthur, from 'MacArtair'. Their traditional lands were in Lorne in Argyll. Isabel Arthur, from Edinburgh, emigrated to Philadelphia in 1775, and Duncan McArthur from Jura settled in North Carolina in 1754. Linked with the Clan Campbell or the Clan MacArthur.

AUCHENLECK, sometimes modified to AFFLECK. Derived from Auchenleck in Ayrshire or Affleck in Angus. A Gaelic place name meaning '*field of the flat stone*'. Thomas Auchenleck sailed from Dundee via London to the Chesapeake in 1628, and Thomas Affleck was a merchant in South Carolina before 1758.

AUCHMUTY. Dating from the thirteenth century the name is territorial based on a place in Fife. The Gaelic prefix '*auch*' means '*field*'. The Auchmuties were among the Undertakers of the Plantation of Ulster in 1610. Robert Auchmuty, Admiralty Court Judge of New England, died in 1750.

AULD. Descriptive, meaning 'old' from Old English. A surname in Scotland since the thirteenth century. John Auld, a Jacobite drummer-boy, was transported to the colonies in 1747.

AUSTIN. Either a diminutive of Augustine or an Anglicisation of the Gaelic name 'Uisdean'. Adam Austin, a merchant from Perthshire, settled in Charleston before 1782, and Isobel Astine emigrated to Philadelphia in 1775..

AYTON, AITON, EATON. Originating as the town on the river Eye in Berwickshire. Used as a surname since the twefth century. Thomas Eaton, from Edinburgh, emigrated to Philadelphia in 1774.

BADENOCH. Territorial, a Gaelic place name, meaning '*marshy land*'. Specifically a district of Inverness-shire. George

Badenoch, a cattle rustler from Perthshire, was transported to the colonies in 1772.

BAILLIE. Occupational, from the Old French word *'baillif'* meaning 'a justice'. It has been used as a surname in Scotland since the early fourteenth century. A family of gypsies bearing the name Baillie was transported to New York in 1682. Scottish Baillies were among the first settlers of Georgia. Hugh Baillie emigrated from Belfast to Philadelphia in 1773.

BAIN, BANE. Descriptive. From the Gaelic word *'ban'* meaning 'fair'. Several Bains were transported as Jacobites to the American Plantations in 1716 and in 1746. Some Bains are affiliated to the Clan Mackay, and other to Clan MacBain.

BAIRD. Probably territorial. As early as the twefth century there were 'de Bardes' living in Lanarkshire. Robert Baird was a merchant in Surinam in 1689, William Baird, a Jacobite, was transported to the Chesapeake in 1747. Clan Baird.

BALD. This may be either a descriptive surname or a diminutive of an Anglo-Saxon forename. Examples date from the thirteenth century. William Bald, a Glasgow wright, emigrated to New York in 1775.

BALDRIDGE. Possibly (1) from the Old English name *'Baeldred'*, or (2) a Gaelic placename bearing the prefix *'bal'* meaning 'town'. Extremely rare. Daniel Baldridge was in Philadelphia during 1762.

BALFOUR. The prefix 'Bal' comes from the Gaelic *'Baile'* meaning town. A Gaelic placename from Fife later the barony of Balfour in the parish of Markinch. The earliest example is John de Balfure in 1304. William Balfour died in Virginia before 1686; John Balfour, a planter and merchant in South Carolina, before 1781; Janet Balfour from Edinburgh emigrated to Philadelphia in 1775.

BALLANTYNE. A place name, using the Gaelic prefix *'baile'* meaning 'township', probably from Bellenden in Lanarkshire, possibly from Ballintome in Stirlingshire. Thomas Ballantine, from Dundee, emigrated to Philadelphia in 1775.

BALMAINE. Territorial, a Gaelic name from the land of Balmain in Kincardineshire. Relatively rare. Alexander Balmain, a minister, settled in Virginia in 1772, and Alexander Bullman (!) was in Boston by 1694.

BALNEAVES. Territorial, derived from lands in Angus, based on a Gaelic placename with the prefix *bal'*. An uncommon surname with early examples in Angus and Fife dating from the sixteenth century. Reverend William Balneavis settled in Antigua in 1712.

BALVERD. Territorial, derived from Balvaird in Fife. Used as a surname since the sixteenth century. James Balverd, a sailor from Dundee, settled in South Carolina around 1729.

BAND. A variant of 'Bond' a term for a peasant. James Band was in Boston by 1686.

BANKS. A surname of unclear origin, traditionally localised in Orkney or Edinburgh. Joseph Banks, from Edinburgh, settled in Jamaica during 1721, and James Banks served in the Pennsylvania Regiment of 1759.

BANNATYNE. Territorial, from an unidentified Gaelic placename. Examples date back to the twelfth century, George and John Bannatyne, two Covenanters from Craigmuir, were banished to the American Plantations in 1684. Clan Campbell.

BANNERMAN. Believed to be an occupational name signifying one who carried the banner or standard, ie the flag-bearer. Traditionally found in north-east Scotland. Mark Bannerman, a Jacobite, was transported to St Kitts in 1716. Bannerman is a sept of the Clan Forbes.

BARCLAY. Although possibly English in origin the name has been used in Scotland since the twefth century. Most early examples come from north-east Scotland. John Barclay, from Kincardineshire, settled in East New Jersey in 1684, Reverend Thomas Barclay emigrated to Albany in 1707, and Alexander Barclay, a customs controller, died in Philadelphia in 1770. Clan Barclay.

BARNHILL. A descriptive surname indicated a place of residence – the barn on the hill. Possibly from Barnhill near Dundee. James Barnhill from Renfrewshire was in Boston by 1759.

BARR. A name of territorial origin from one or more places in southwest Scotland, probably derived from the Gaelic for 'height'. Examples date from the fifteenth century. Andrew Barr emigrated from Leith to Philadelphia in 1775, and Samuel Barr, emigrated from Belfast to Philadelphia in 1773.

BARRON, BARON. A baron is the lowest level of chivalry and held a barony – a small estate – from the Crown. Reverend Robert Baron settled in Bermuda in 1700 later moving to Maryland.

BARRY, BARRIE. In Scotland this name is derived from the parish of Barry in Angus. Most early examples come from eastern Scotland. Two Jacobites named Barry were transported in 1716, one to South Carolina and the other to Maryland.

BARTON. A surname, meaning *'barley-settlement'*, recorded in Scotland since the thirteenth century. Walter Barton was in Boston by 1686.

BAXTER. From the Old English word *'bachster'* for a baker. Examples of this surname exist from the thirteenth century. Alexander Baxter, a Glasgow butcher, emigrated to New York in 1774. Some Baxters claim to be septs of the Clan MacMillan.

BEAN. From the Gaelic *'beathan'* meaning 'life'. Several Jacobite Beans were transported to the West Indies in 1716 and 1747, Alexander Bean, a shoemaker, settled in Georgia in 1775, and John Bean emigrated from Belfast to Philadelphia in 1773. Part of the Clan MacBain.

BEATON. Territorial, probably derived from Bethune a town in northern France. Recorded in Scotland since the twelfth century. Some are linked with the MacDonalds, others with the MacLeods, and a number with the MacLeans. Mary Beaton settled on the Argyle Patent, New York, by 1763, and Angus Bethune, a Loyalist, moved from New York to Quebec. Clans Donald, MacLeod or MacLean.

BEATTIE, BEATTY. Possibly a diminutive of the name Bartholemew. Historically the name is found from the Borders north along the east coast as far as Aberdeen, and also in Ulster. John Beatty, a minister educated at Glasgow University, settled in Virginia in 1732, while William Beatty from Galloway emigrated to New York in 1774.

BEGBIE. Possibly derived from a place name of Scandinavian origin as it has the suffix 'bie' signifying 'settlement'. John Bagby, a Jacobite, was transported to South Carolina in 1716, and William Begbie was a shipwright on the Wando River, South Carolina, in 1769..

BELL. A name with a number of possible derivations, possibly from *'Le Bel'* (Old French for handsome) or from the English word 'bell' indicating an occupation or place of origin. The greatest concentration of the family seem to have been on the Borders, particularly in Dumfries-shire. The Bells were among the Border reiver families of the sixteenth century. In the seventeenth century a number of them settled in Ireland and today Bell is one of the commonest surnames in County Antrim and County Down. Alexander Bell, a merchant from Glasgow, settled in West Florida before 1777, while Alison Bell was transported to New York in 1682. Some Bells claim to be a sept of the MacMillans.

BENNET. A diminutive of Benedict. Examples as a surname occur in Scotland from the fifteenth century onwards. William Bennet, a forger from Roxburghshire, was banished to the American Plantations in 1751, while another William Bennet, a carpenter on the Dolphin, died in North America during 1699.

BENNY. Territorial, probably from Bennie in Perthshire, originally *'Beinnach'* a Gaelic place-name meaning 'hilly place'. A surname used since around 1200 AD. Agnes Benny settled in East New Jersey in 1684.

BERRY. Possibly of Flemish origin. James Berry, a clockmaker from Queensferry, emigrated to Philadelphia in 1775, and John Berry, a schoolmaster from Aberdeen, settled in Maryland in 1735.

BERTRAM, BARTRAM. A variation of the Old English name *'Beorhtram'* meaning 'shining raven'. The name has been recorded in Scotland since the late thirteenth century. Alexander Bartram, a merchant from Lanarkshire, settled in Philadelphia before the American Revolution.

BERWICK. Territorial, derived from the burgh of Berwick, based on the Old English words *'bere'* meaning 'barley' and *'wic'* meaning 'settlement'. Recorded as a surname in Scotland since the thirteenth century. Andrew Berwick emigrated to Jamaica in 1730.

BETHUNE, (see Beaton above) Angus Bethune settled in New York before 1776, and George Bethune was a banker in Boston by 1724. Clan Donald.

BEVERIDGE. A name from Fife and Lothian since the early fourteenth century. John Beveridge, a Covenanter, was transported to East New Jersey in 1685, and Hendry Beveridge, a mariner, visited New England and Nova Scotia by 1624.

BEVERLEY. Territorial, probably from the town of Beverley in Yorkshire, England. Found in Scotland from the late thirteenth century onwards. John and William Beverley, both Jacobites from Aberdeen, were transported to Maryland in 1747.

BIGGAM. Territorial, derived from lands of Bigholm or Bigham in Ayrshire or Dumfries-shire. Most of the early examples come from

Edinburgh. William Biggam from Galloway emigrated to New York in 1774.

BIGGAR. Territorial, originating in the parish of Biggar in Lanarkshire, and used as a surname since the twelfth century. John Biggar, a tailor, emigrated to New York in 1774.

BINNING. Territorial, taken from a place name in Whitekirk near Haddington, and used as a surname since the thirteenth century. John Binning was in Boston by 1702

BIRRELL, BURREL. Examples date from 1387 in Northumberland, England, and later in Berwick, Scotland. James Birrell, from Fife, died on the Darien Expedition of 1698.

BISHOP. Presumably from the office of bishop. Dating from the thirteenth century as a surname. Peter Bishop, from Paisley, was banished to America in 1767.

BISSETT. A Norman French name introduced into Scotland during the twelfth century. Many of the early examples come from north east Scotland. Andrew Bisset settled in New York by 1712, and William Bissett was a tailor in Charleston before 1754. Clan Bissett..

BLACK, BLAKE. An Old English surname of descriptive origin. It exists in a Latin form in medieval Scots manuscripts, for example Hugh Niger in Angus 1178. In its present form there are examples dating from the fourteenth century. Thomas Blake, a Scots merchant, accompanied Coronado on his expedition through what is now the American southwest during the mid-sixteenth century, and Daniel Black a Cromwellian prisoner of war, was shipped to Boston in 1651. Blacks may be allied to the MacLeans, the Lamonts or the MacGregors.

BLACKADDER. Territorial, derived from the lands of Blackadder in Berwickshire. The family of Blackadder of that Ilk is noted in 1426. Thomas Blackadder was a merchant in late seventeenth century New England.

BLACKBURN. Territorial, derived from one or more places of that name, meaning 'dark stream'. Examples date from the mid thirteenth century onwards. John Blackburn, a merchant from Glasgow, settled in Norfolk, Virginia, around 1750.

BLACKHALL. Territorial, derived from the lands of Blackhall in Aberdeenshire. Most early examples come from the district of Garioch. Agnes Blackhall emigrated to New York in 1774.

BLACKIE, BLAIKIE. A diminutive of Black or Blake recorded in
Lowland Scotland since the sixteenth century. Charles Blackie and
his family sailed for Prince Edward Island in 1775 from
Kirkcudbright.

BLACKLOCK. Descriptive, a Cumbrian surname meaning *'one with
black hair'*. Found in south west Scotland since the fifteenth
century. William Blacklock, from Dumfries, emigrated to
Charleston in 1774, and John Blacklock was in Boston by 1687.

BLACKSTOCK. Probably a territorial surname, one which has been
recorded since the fifteenth century mainly in the south west. James
Blackstock was in Boston by 1715.

BLACKTON. Territorial, derived from a place of that name.
Uncommon. Hannah Blackton, from Edinburgh, emigrated to
Philadelphia in 1775.

BLACKWOOD. A territorial surname dating from the fourteenth century,
based on places in south west Scotland. Robert Blackwood, an
Edinburgh merchant, owned land in East New Jersey around 1685,
while John Blackwood from Lanarkshire, settled in Canada in 1780.

BLAIN, BLANE, MACBLANE. Surnames of Gaelic origin found in
Ayr and Galloway. Patrick Blain, a farmer from Galloway,
emigrated to New York in 1774.

BLAIR. Derived from the Gaelic *'blar'* meaning 'field', it has been a
surname in Scotland since the early thirteenth century and in Ulster
since the days of the Plantation. Reverend James Blair, from
Banffshire, was the Commissary of Virginia and founder of the
College of William and Mary, while John Blair, a thief, was
transported to Barbados in 1653, and James Blair emigrated from
Larne to Charleston in 1773.

BLUE. A name of Gaelic origin found in Argyll. A number of Blues
emigrated from Jura and Knapdale to North Carolina in the
eighteenth century.

BOAG, BOIG, BOOG. Origin unclear, may be territorial. John Boag
from Orkney settled in Jamaica during 1733, and a John Boog
emigrated to New York in 1774.

BOATH. Territorial, from the lands of Both in Angus. Possibly from the
Gaelic *'both'* meaning 'house'. Elizabeth Boath emigrated to New
York in 1774.

BOGLE. Territorial, derived from a place in Lanarkshire. Most of the early examples come from Glasgow. Alexander Bogle was a member of the Scots Charitable Society of Boston in 1657, and Robert Bogle emigrated to Jamaica in 1773.

BONTEIN, BUNTEN. Origins unclear but may be linked to the English family Bunting. Recorded in Scotland since the thirteenth century. Most early examples come from Dunbartonshire. James Buntine emigrated to Jamaica in 1773.

BONTHRON. A surname of unknown origin found mainly in Fife. Examples date from the seventeenth century. James Bonthron sailed to Darien in 1698

BORLAND, BORELAND. From a number of places of that name in Lowland Scotland. Reverend Francis Borland served in Surinam, Barbados and Darien, while John Borland was a merchant in Boston, both in the late seventeenth century

BORTHWICK. Territorial, derived from the barony of Borthwick on the Borders. Possibly an Old English placename as it has the suffix *'wick'* indicating 'farmstead'. Used as a surname in Scotland since the fourteenth century. James Borthwick was transported to Virginia before 1733, and William Borthwick was in Boston by 1717.

BOSWELL A Norman French territorial surname introduced into Scotland in the twelfth century. Dr James Boswell died in Montserrat in 1767.

BOTHWELL. Territorial, derived from Bothwell in Lanarkshire. An Old English place name meaning 'hut by the fishpool'. Used as a surname in Scotland since around 1200. John Bothwell, from Aberdeen, died in Charleston by 1777.

BOWDEN. Territorial, originating in the lands of Bowden in Roxburghshire. Probably derived from a Gaelic term *'both an duin'* meaning 'the house on the hill. Used as a surname since around 1200 AD. James Bouden was in Boston by 1697.

BOWIE, BUIE. A descriptive name from the Gaelic word *buidhe* meaning 'yellow' or 'fair'. Donald Buie, a smith from Jura, settled in North Carolina in 1754, and Reverend John Bowie settled in Maryland in 1771. Buie is a sept of Clan Donald.

BOWMAN. Possibly a Territorial surname based on Beaumont in France and introduced into Scotland by the Anglo-Normans in the twelfth century. As Bowman it is recorded in the thirteenth century and later, whereas Beaumont or variant is rare. Christian Bowman was transported to the American Plantations in 1695, and Archibald Bowman emigrated to Boston in 1768.

BOYCE. From the French word '*bois*' meaning wood. It appears in Scottish documents as early as the twefth century. Janet Boyce, a spinner from Paisley, emigrated to New York in 1774.

BOYD. Possibly territorial and derived from '*Bhoid*' the Gaelic term for the island of Bute. Early references come from Renfrewshire-Ayrshire. Reverend Andrew Boyd settled in Virginia in 1709 and Spencer Boyd was a merchant in King and Queen County, Virginia, by 1770.

BOYLE. A Norman-French name, originating in Beauville, France, which was introduced into Scotland in the medieval period. John Boyle settled in St Croix before 1777, while Alexander Boyle was the Surveyor General of New York in 1691, and Susanna Boyle emigrated from Belfast to Philadelphia in 1773.

BRABAND. Territorial, derived from Brabant in Flanders. A very rare surname in Scotland. Alexander Braband was a prisoner of war transported to New England in 1650.

BRACKENRIDGE. Territorial, derived from the lands of Brackenrig in Lanarkshire. Examples date from the fifteenth century. Hugh Henry Brackenridge, from Argyll, graduated from Princeton in 1771.

BRADLEY. Territorial derived from the lands of Braidlie in Hawick, Roxburghshire. A surname since the thirteenth century. Charles Bradley, a rioter from Greenock, was transported to the colonies in 1773.

BRADNER. A variant of 'Brander' (see below). Reverend John Bradner emigrated to America by 1715.

BRADY. A diminutive of an Irish Gaelic surname, originally '*MacBradaigh*', found in Scotland since the fifteenth century. John Brady emigrated from Islay to New York in 1740.

BRAIDFOOT, BROADFOOT. Territorial, derived from a place of that name in south west Scotland. Recorded as a surname since the fourteenth century. Reverend James Braidfoot settled in Virginia during 1772.

BRAIDWOOD. From Braidwood in Avondale, Lanarkshire. James Braidwood, a Covenanter, was banished to the West Indies in 1678.

BRAN. A Gaelic forename *'Bran'* meaning 'raven' which was adopted as a surname. Examples date from the seventeenth century. Alexander Bran was in Boston by 1733.

BRAND. Probably a name of Scandinavian origin. Relatively uncommon but found in Scotland since the fourteenth century. James Brand, a Jacobite, was transported to the Chesapeake in 1747.

BRANDER. An occupational surname signifying 'grid-iron smith'. Adam Brander, a carpenter, settled in Jamaica in 1774, and Laurence Brander died in New York by July 1768.

BRANDON. Territorial, based on a place name in northern England. Examples date from Angus in the seventeenth century. John Brandon emigrated to Boston in 1716.

BREBNER. A corruption of Brabander, i.e. a native of Brabant in Flanders. People, particularly textile workers, from there settled in medieval Scotland bringing industrial skills such as weaving. Brebner became virtually synonymous with weaver. Alexander Brebner, from Aberdeenshire, settled in St Croix before 1775, and James Brebner, also from Aberdeen, was a judge in Grenada during the mid-eighteenth century.

BRECHIN. Territorial, derived from the burgh of Brechin in Angus, and used as a surname since the twelfth century. Reverend James Brechin settled in Virginia in 1702.

BREMNER. A variation of Brebner, (see above). William Bremner, from Orkney, settled in Georgia in 1775, and George Bremner, a farmer soldier, settled in Albany County, New York, in 1767 but moved to Canada by 1782.

BRICE. BRYCE. A forename and later a surname in medieval Scotland. Three Covenanters named Bryce were banished to the American Plantations in the seventeenth century.

BRIGG, BRIGGS. In Scots *'brig'* is the equivalent of *'bridge'* in English thus the name may indicate the location of residence. Samuel Briggs settled in Friendsborough, Georgia, in 1774.

BRISBANE. A surname introduced from England in the late thirteenth century. Matthew Brisbane was transported to Barbados in 1674, and Robert Brisbane, from Glasgow, settled in Charleston in 1733.

BROCK. Territorial, derived from a place name in Renfrewshire. A surname in Scotland since the fourteenth century. Walter Brock, a Glasgow merchant, emigrated to New York in 1775, and Robert Broke was an indentured servant in Charleston in 1733.

BRODIE, BRODY. Probably of Gaelic origin. Originating in the barony of Brodie in Morayshire. Examples date from the early fourteenth century. Reverend Brody was sent to Virginia in 1709, John Brodie, a Jacobite, was transported to Virginia in 1747, and another John Brodie emigrated to Georgia in 1737. Brodie may be linked with the Clan Donald.

BROTHERSTONE. Territorial, derived from the lands of Brothirstanys, in East Lothian, and based on the Old English words '*Brothor's tun*' meaning the 'settlement of Brothor'. Examples of the surname date back to the mid twelfth century. Alexander Brotherton, a Loyalist in Albany, New York, moved to New Brunswick by 1786.

BROUGH. Probably derived from the Scandinavian word '*borg*' or the Old English word '*burg*' both indicating a fort, alternatively from the Gaelic '*bruach*' meaning slope. George Brough, from Orkney, settled in Richmond County, Georgia, in 1774.

BROWN. Descriptive from the Old English word '*brun*'. One of the most common names in Scotland. Scottish Browns were found throughout the American colonies. Gustavus Brown was a physician in Portobacco, Maryland, up to his death in 1762, Hugh Brown, one of the founders of the Scottish Carolina Company, settled there from 1684 to 1690, and Peter Brown, a Dundee carpenter, sailed for Cape Fear in 1752. Some Browns claim allegiance to the Clan Lamont.

BROWNHILL. Derived from several place-names in Scotland. Examples date back to the fourteenth century. Thomas Brownhill, a Jacobite from Perthshire, was transported to the West Indies in 1747, and Henry Brounell was transported to New England in 1651.

BROWNING. A diminutive of 'Brown' used in Scotland since the fourteenth century. James Browning emigrated to New England in 1720.

BROWNLEE, BROWNLIE. Territorial, probably based on Brownlee in Lanarkshire and possibly from Brownlee in Ayrshire. As a surname it has been in use since the sixteenth century. Robert Brownlie emigrated to New York in 1775.

BRUCE. A Norman French surname derived from Brix in Normandy and taken to England at the time of the Conquest. David I, impressed by the feudal system introduced into England by the Normans, encouraged Anglo-Norman knights to settle in Scotland. One such was Robert de Brus who was granted lands in Annandale. Robert Bruce, a Jacobite, was transported to Virginia in 1716, while James and George Bruce were indentured in Chester County, Pennsylvania, during 1697.

BRUNTON. Territorial, from a number of places of that name in Scotland. Examples date from the sixteenth century. Janet Bruntoun emigrated to New York in 1682 and Grizel Brunton from Perth went to Salem in 1775.

BRYCE. Originating with St Bricius, a medieval French saint. Initially a personal name but used as a surname since the thirteenth century. John Bryce, a Covenanter, was deported to Virginia in 1668, and another John Brice, a Jacobite, was transported to the American Colonies in 1747.

BRYSON. Patronymic, meaning son of Brice. Examples date from the fourteenth century. Emigrants include James Bryson who sailed to New York in 1774.

BUCHAN. Territorial, from the district of Buchan in Aberdeenshire. Buchan has been used as a surname from the thirteenth century. Thomas Buchan, a farmer, sailed to New York in 1774, and Alexander Buchan was an indentured servant imported into East New Jersey in 1684. Buchan may be a sept of the Clan Comyn.

BUCHANAN. Territorial, derived from the district of Buchanan in Stirlingshire. Based on the Gaelic 'both chanain' meaning 'house of the canon'. Used as a surname since the thirteenth century. James Buchanan settled in Nova Scotia in 1628, David Buchanan, a Cromwellian transportee, landed in Boston in 1652, and John Bohannon emigrated from Philadelphia in 1775. Clan Buchanan.

BUDGE. An uncommon surname from Caithness and Orkney which has been used there since the fourteenth century. William Budge settled in Friendsborough, Georgia, in 1775, and William Budge was in Boston by 1732. Clan Donald.

BUIE, BUEA. (See Bowie, above).

BUIST. A surname from Fife, possibly a variation of 'Best'. John Buist from Fife participated in the Darien Expedition of 1698.

BULLOCH. Territorial, based on a place name in Stirlingshire. James Bulloch from Glasgow, settled in Charleston in 1728. Clan Donald.

BURGES, BURGESS. Descriptive, a burgess was a freeman or citizen of a burgh. Used as a surname since the fourteenth century. James Burges, a merchant from Edinburgh, settled in North Carolina in 1775, and Alexander Burgess was transported to New England in 1650.

BURN. From the Middle English word *burne* meaning 'brook' or 'stream'. From a number of sources in Scotland. Two Jacobites named John Burn were transported in 1716, one to Virginia and the other to South Carolina.

BURNETT. Believed to have derived from the Old Norse name *Beornheard*, which became 'Burnard' then 'Burnet'. Early examples of the surnames come from the eastern Borders and by the fourteenth century the north east of Scotland. John Burnett, a merchant from Aberdeen, was trading in Virginia in 1638 and Dr William Burnet settled in West Florida before the American Revolution. Some Burnetts are connected with the Clan Campbell.

BURNS. Originally this was 'Burnhouse' becoming 'Burness' and finally 'Burns'. John Burns settled in New York in 1774, and John Burns emigrated to New England in 1736. Burns and Burness are recognized septs of Clan Campbell.

BURNSIDE. A name of several settlements in Scotland indicating a place at the side of a stream. Examples date from the sixteenth century. Harry Burnside emigrated to New York in 1774.

BURT, BURD. A surname found originally in Fife. Two Burts sailed for Darien in 1698 and a Patrick Burt, from Perth, died in South Carolina before 1776. James Burd settled in Lancaster, Pennsylvania, by 1771.

BURTON. From the Anglo-Saxon meaning 'the farmers town'. William Burton, a merchant, landed in Boston in 1763.

BUTTER. An uncommon surname dating from the the fourteenth century, mainly found in Perthshire. William Butter, a coppersmith from Perth, emigrated to Philadelphia in 1775.

BYRES. Territorial, derived from the old barony of Byres in East Lothian a property long owned by the Lindsay of the Byres family. Early examples of the surname tend to come from south east Scotland. Margaret Byres, from Edinburgh, was banished to the American Plantations in 1697.

CADDELL. A variant of Calder, see below, recorded in Scotland since the sixteenth century. Christian Caddell was transported to Barbados in 1663, and Robert Caddell was in Boston by 1733. Some Caddells are linked to Clan Campbell.

CADDIE. Territorial, derived from the old Barony of Cadzow in Lanarkshire. The earliest example is a W. de Cadio a canon of Glasgow in 1258. James Caddie, a farmer from Montrose, sailed for New York in 1775.

CAIRNS. Territorial, derived from Cairns in Midlothian, dating from at least the mid fourteenth century. Found also in Ulster from 1610 when Alexander Cairns from Wigtonshire settled in Donegal. John Carnes was admitted as a member of the Scots Charitable Society of Boston in 1696, David and Jane Cairns settled in Quebec in 1774, and John Cairns emigrated from Belfast to Philadelphia in 1771.

CALDCLEUGH. A surname taken from a place of that name in Teviothead, Roxburghshire, with examples dating from the sixteenth century. Andrew Caldcleugh settled in America before 1776.

CALDER. A territorial name, probably from the Gaelic *'call dobhar'* or 'hazel stream', but possibly from Norse *'kalfadal'* meaning 'calf's valley'. Recorded as a surname as early as the twelfth century in Scotland. Alexander Calder and his family emigrated to Savanna, Georgia, in 1775, and Robert Calder was in Boston by 1719. Linked with Clan Campbell.

CALDERWOOD. Territorial, derived from a place-name in Lanarkshire. Used as a surname since the thirteenth century. John Calderwood was transported to the American Plantations in 1667, and James Calderwood emigrated from Londonderry to New Hampshire in 1725.

CALDWELL. Territorial, based on a place-name in Renfrewshire. As a surname it dates from the fourteenth century. Mr William Caldwell is recorded in Virginia during 1646, and Donald Caldwell emigrated to North Carolina in 1774.

CALLAN. An abbreviation of MacAllan (see below). Examples date from the seventeenth century. Alexander Callan emigrated to North Carolina in 1774. Clan Donald.

CALLANDAR, CALLENDER. Territorial, from the barony of Callander in Perthshire. Used as a surname since the thirteenth century. Three Royalist prisoners-of-war named Callendar were transported to New England by Oliver Cromwell in 1651.

CALLUM. An abbreviation of Malcolm or MacCallum, (see below). James Callum, a Covenanter, was banished to the Plantations after 1666 and died in Carolina.

CAMERON. The Highland Camerons have a descriptive Gaelic surname *'cam-shron'* meaning 'hooked nose' whereas the Lowland Camerons are likely to have a territorial name from the parish of Cameron in Fife. The main Cameron lands were in Inverness-shire. Sir Ewan Cameron of Lochiel purchased land in East New Jersey in 1685, while a number of Jacobite Camerons were transported to America after 1747. Clan Cameron.

CAMPBELL. This is a descriptive Gaelic surname *'caimbeul'* meaning 'crooked or wry mouth'. A surname traditionally associated with Argyllshire and parts of neighboring Perthshire. The name is also common in Ulster although not all Campbells there are of Scottish origin. Campbells could be found in virtually every British colony in America before 1776. Clan Campbell.

CANDOW. Possibly from the Gaelic *'Ceann-dhu'* meaning 'black-head'. Donald Candow, a Jacobite prisoner-of-war, was transported to the colonies in 1746.

CANNON. Recorded in Galloway since the sixteenth century. Samuel Cannon, a Covenanter from Kirkcudbright, was banished to America in 1684, and James Cannon was a professor at the University of Pennsylvania before 1782.

CANT. A name found in eastern Scotland since the medieval period and thought to be of Flemish origin. James Cant was a merchant in Virginia by the 1650s, and Catherine Cant emigrated to Philadelphia in 1775.

CANTLIE. Territorial, derived from a place in Yorkshire. Used as a surname in Scotland since the mid fifteenth century. Alexander Cantlie emigrated to Jamaica in 1730.

CARDNO. Territorial, derived from the lands of Cardno near Fraserburgh, Aberdeenshire. It contains the Gaelic prefix *'cathair'* meaning fort. Alexander Cardno, from Peterhead, fled to Virginia in 1679.

CARGILL. From the lands of Cargill in Strathmore. The prefix 'car' comes from the Gaelic *'cathair'* meaning 'fort'. As a surname it dates back to the thirteenth century. Historically the surname was found in Perthshire and Angus. William Cargill, a Jacobite from Montrose, was transported to Maryland in 1747, and two Cargills from Jura settled in North Carolina in 1754.

CARLE. An Anglo-Saxon name, originally *'ceorl'* meaning 'countryman'. A surname found in north east Scotland. Robert Carle was in Boston by 1697.

CARLYLE, CARLISLE. From Carlisle in Cumberland. Used as a surname in Scotland since the twefth century. Adam and Alexander Carlyle, from Lanarkshire, were merchant planters in Virginia in the 1740s.

CARMICHAEL. Derived from the barony of Carmichael in Lanarkshire and in use as a surname since the thirteenth century. A group of Carmichaels from Perthshire emigrated to North Carolina in 1775. Some Carmichaels are linked with the MacDougalls.

CARNEGIE. Territorial, based on the Gaelic *'cathair an eige'* meaning 'fort at the gap'. Dating as a surname from the mid-fourteenth century and originating in the barony of Carnegie in Angus. John Carnegie, a minister in Virginia, died in 1709, and James Carnegie settled in Charleston by 1721. Clan Carnegie.

CARNOCHAN. Territorial, taken from Carnochan in Ayrshire Possibly from the Gaelic word *'carnach'* meaning 'a rocky place'. Relatively uncommon, but mainly found in Galloway. Edmond Carnochan was banished to Barbados in 1685.

CARR, CAR. A variation of Kerr. Found in east central Scotland from the fifteenth century onwards. Alexander Carr, a Jacobite, was transported to Virginia in 1716, James Carr emigrated from Belfast to Philadelphia in 1773.

CARRICK. Territorial, originating in the district of Carrick in Ayrshire. James Carrick, a merchant, settled in Boston by 1754, and Richard Carrick was in Virginia by 1650.

CARRIE, CARRY. Possibly an abbreviation of MacCarra or MacCairre, or a variant of Carey. John Carrie, a Jacobite, was transported to Maryland in 1747, and John Carry, a mason, emigrated to Virginia in 1773.

CARRON. Territorial, taken from Carron in Stirlingshire. Possibly from the Gaelic *'car abhuinn'* meaning ' winding river'. A surname recorded since the seventeenth century. Richard Carron, a Jacobite, was banished to Antigua in 1747.

CARRUTHERS. Territorial, derived from the lands of Carruthers in Dumfries-shire. A British place name bearing the prefix *'caer'* meaning 'fort'. A surname in use since the thirteenth century. John Carruthers died in Craven County, North Carolina, in 1751.

CARSON, CORSAN. An old surname from Galloway in south-west Scotland. Used as early as the twelfth century. Carsons were among the Scots who settled in Ulster during the seventeenth century. Several Carsons sailed from Scotland bound for America in the early 1770s.

CASKIE. An abbreviation of *'MacCaskie'*, used as a surname since the seventeenth century. William Caskie sailed to Darien in 1698. Clan McLeod.

CASSELS, CASSILLS, Probably from Cassillis in Ayrshire, and derived from the Gaelic worh *'caiseal'* meaning 'fort'. John and Isobel Cassels, from Edinburgh, emigrated to Philadelphia in 1775.

CATHCART. An old surname derived from the land of Cathcart near Glasgow. Derived from the British term meaning 'fort on the (river) Cart'. Ranald of Cathcart was possibly a Breton who settled in Scotland in the twelfth century. Andrew Cathcart, a merchant, sailed from Ayr bound for the West Indies in 1681, and William Cathcart, a physician, emigrated to South Carolina in 1737.

CATTENACH. A Gaelic term signifying 'of the (clan) Chattan'. A name found in Highland Aberdeenshire. John Cattenach, a farmer from Caithness, was aboard the Bachelor of Leith which sailed for North Carolina in 1774. Cattenach is a sept of Clan MacPherson.

CAVERS. Territorial, from Cavers in Roxburghshire. Relatively uncommon, early examples of the surname comes from south-east

Scotland. John Cavers, a Covenanter, was transported to the West Indies in 1675.

CAVIE. A surname of unknown origin recorded in Scotland since the fifteenth century. Christian Cavy, a Covenanter, was banished to the American Plantations in 1685.

CAW. Probably a diminutive of MacCaw. Thomas Caw died in Charleston in 1773, and John Caw, a Jacobite, was transported to the American colonies in 1747.

CHALMERS, CHAMBERS. A variant of an Old French word *chambre* meaning chamber and later, by extension, chamberlain. It is therefore a name of occupational origin meaning court official or treasurer. Examples date from the thirteenth century. Several Chalmers and Chambers were transported to the American colonies for participating in the Jacobite Rebellions of 1715 and 1745. John Chambers emigrated from Belfast to Philadelphia in 1773. Some Chalmers or Chambers are affiliated with the Clan Campbell.

CHAPLIN. From the occupation of chaplain, and used as a surname since the medieval period. George and Robert Chaplin, both from north east Scotland, settled as merchants in Jamaica in the early eighteenth century.

CHAPMAN. Occupational, from the Old English word for merchant or pedlar. The earliest recording was in Dundee in 1296. James Chapman, a gardener and a Jacobite from Banff, was transported to Maryland in 1747, and David Chapman, a thief, was transported to Darien in 1698.

CHAPP, CHEAP. A rare name, possibly from the Old English word for a trader. Found in east central Scotland. James Chapp, a Jacobite, was exiled to Maryland in 1747, and Patrick Cheap was in Boston in 1712.

CHARTERIS, CHARTERS. A territorial suname derived from the French town of Chartres. A surname introduced into Scotland by the thirteenth century. William Charters was in Boston by 1705.

CHATTO. Derived from lands of that name in Roxburghshire. Examples date back 800 years. William Chatto, a saddler from Kelso, was transported to the colonies in 1769.

CHEYNE. A Norman-French name introduced into Scotland around 1200, probably territorial from Quesney near Cotances. Mostly found in north east Scotland. John Cheyne was transported to Boston in 1651. Cheyne is a sept of Clan Sutherland.

CHISHOLM. Territorial from the barony of Chisholm in Roxburghshire. Early examples of the surname come from the eastern Borders but by the mid fourteenth century a branch of the family settled in Inverness-shire and in Gaelic were known as *'An Siosalach Glaiseach'*. Some Jacobite Chisholms were banished to Jamaica in the eighteenth century, while Thomas Chisholm, a farmer from Kirkcudbrightshire, settled on Prince Edward Island in 1775. Clan Chisholm.

CHRISTIE, CHRISTY. Possibly an abbreviation of Christopher. Most commonly found in Fife where it can be traced back to the fifteenth century. Robert Christie, a merchant from Culross, wrote from Florida in 1667 of his intention to go to Mexico.

CLAPERTON. Territorial in origin, recorded since the sixteenth century. Two Clapertons were banished as Jacobites in 1747, Thomas to Maryland and his son William to the Leeward Islands.

CLARK, CLERK. Occupational in origin, first as a member of a religious order and later as a scribe. Examples date from the late thirteenth century. A common surname throughout Scotland and Ulster. Archibald Clark from Jura emigrated to North Carolina in 1754 and James Clark, a merchant, settled in Virginia by 1754. Clarks or Clerks are generally septs of the MacPhersons or the Mackintoshes.

CLARKSON. Patronymic meaning 'son of the clerk'. James Clarkson, a Covenanter and merchant, sailed to Carolina in 1684, later settled in East New Jersey. Some claim to be part of the Clan MacPherson and others of the Clan Cameron.

CLAYTON. Probably a territorial surname. In Angus the surname appears as 'Cleatoun' during the seventeenth century. John Clayton emigrated to North Carolina in 1739.

CLEGHORN. From the lands of Cleghorn in Lanarkshire. Possibly derived from the Old English *'claeg erne'* meaning 'clay house'. Adam Cleghorn is recorded in New York by 1699, and James Cleghorn, a Cromwellian prisoner, was transported to New England by 1650.

CLELAND. From the lands of Cleland or Kneland in Lanarkshire. Used in Scotland as a surname since the thirteenth century. James

Cleland, a surgeon apothecary from Lanarkshire, emigrated to Jamaica in 1735, and William Cleland, a merchant from Edinburgh, died in Barbados during 1719. Three Kneelands were members of the Scots Charitable Society of Boston in the seventeenth century.

CLEPHANE. An Anglo-Norman name first recorded in Scotland during the twefth century. Reverend David Clephane settled in Virginia around 1709.

CLOUSTON, CLEWSTON. Territorial, derived from a place name in Orkney and based on an Old Norse term *'klostadr'*. Used as a surname in the Orkney Islands since around 1500. William Clewston was deported by Cromwell to Boston in 1652, while George Clouston arrived in Pennsylvania during 1698. Clan Sinclair.

CLYDE. An uncommon surname in Scotland dating from the fifteenth century. Daniel Clyde emigrated via Ireland to New England in 1730, and Thomas Clyde left Belfast bound for Philadelphia in 1773.

CLYDESDALE. Territorial, meaning the 'valley of the river Clyde'. Uncommon but recorded since the thirteenth century. Richard Clydesdale, a pedlar and a Covenanter, was transported to the West Indies in 1678.

COCHRANE. Territorial, from the lands of Cochrane near Paisley. Used as a surname since the thirteenth century. James Cochrane, a soldier, was in Georgia by 1737, David Cochrane, a merchant, settled in Richmond, Virginia, before 1776, and James Cochran from Ulster settled in Pennsylvania by 1730. Some Cochranes are linked to Clan Donald.

COCK. Used in Fife as a surname since the mid-sixteenth century. Reverend Daniel Cock, emigrated to America in 1771, and William Cock landed in Philadelphia in 1745..

COCKBURN. Territorial, derived from the lands of Cockburn in Roxburghshire. It dates from around 1200 as a surname, most examples are found in south east Scotland. Possibly a corruption of the Danish name *'Colbrand'*. John Cockburn, a mason from Kelso, settled in Perth Amboy, East New Jersey, in 1685, and Christine Cockburn was transported to Virginia in 1696.

COFFIE. Possibly from an Irish Gaelic surname *'Cobhthaigh'* meaning 'victorious'. James Coffie was transported to Virginia in 1772.

COLE. Probably a variant of Coull (see below). Alexander Cole was in Boston by 1684.

COLQUHOUN. A surname originating in the mid thirteenth century based on the lands of Colquhoun in Dunbartonshire. The name is Gaelic, *'Coil'* means 'wood' and 'cumhann' means 'narrow', thus 'the narrow wood'. Archibald Colquhoun, a surgeon from Edinburgh, settled in New York prior to 1749, and Walter Colquhoun arrived in South Carolina in 1684. Clan Colquhoun.

COLT. Originating in thirteenth century Perthshire based on the barony of Colt there. The name is probably derived from the Gaelic for 'wood'. Relatively uncommon. Andrew Colt, from Stirlingshire, died in Darien around 1699.

COLTHRED, COLTART. Occupational signifying 'a colt herd', or possibly territorial from a village in Normandy. Traditionally found in the Borders and Galloway. John Colthred settled in Georgia in 1737.

COLVILL, COLVIN. Territorial derived from a village in Normandy. The earliest recording of the surname in Scotland dates from 1159. Colvin is a variant used in Scotland. Archibald Colvill was a planter in Barbados before 1647, Catherine Colven settled in Prince Edward Island in 1775, and Robert Colvin emigrated from Belfast to Philadelphia in 1773.

COMRIE. Territorial, taken from Comrie in Perthshire. Most early recordings of the name were in Perthshire. Alexander Comry, a farmer from Stirling emigrated to New York in 1774.

CONKIE. A abbreviated version of *'McConnochie'* (see below). David Conkie, from Galloway, was in Boston by 1767. Clan Campbell.

CONN, CON. Territorial, derived from the lands of Con in the parish of Montquhitter, Aberdeenshire. Reverend Hugh Conn died in Bladensburg, Virginia, in 1752. Clan Donald.

CONNELL. An abbreviation of McConnell. John Connell, a prisoner of war, was transported to Boston in 1651, and Robert Connell emigrated to New York in 1774. Clan Donald.

COOK. An occupational surname, relatively common in Scotland where it has been used since the twelfth century. Thomas Cook, a Jacobite, was transported to the Chesapeake in 1716, and Isobel Cook, from

Edinburgh, was banished to the colonies in 1695. Some Cooks are linked with Clan Donald.

COOPER, COUPAR, CUPAR. Partly derived from the occupation of cooper and partly from the town of Cupar. Thomas and James Cooper, from Wigtonshire, emigrated to New York in 1775.

COPLAND, COPELAND, COUPLAND. Territorial, derived from a place in Cumberland, used as a surname in Scotland since around 1200. Patrick Copland, born in Aberdeen 1572, settled in Bermuda in 1626, moving to the Bahamas in 1648.

CORBETT. Probably Norman-French in origin. The first of that name in Scotland settled in Teviotdale in the early twefth century. Practically all the earlier recordings of the surname come from south-east Scotland. Andrew and John Corbett, two Covenanters, were banished to East New Jersey in 1685.

CORDINER. Occupational, derived from 'cordwainer' meaning shoemaker. John Cordiner, a merchant from Glasgow, was a member of the Scots Charitable Society of Boston, and died there before 1712.

CORKAN. An Irish Gaelic surname *'O'Corcrain'*, found in Galloway. Catherine Corkan landed in Boston during 1763.

CORMACK. Probably an Anglicised abbreviation of the Gaelic surname *'MacCormaig'* meaning *'son of Cormac'.*. Gilbert and Patrick Cormack were members of the Scots Charitable Society of Boston in the late seventeenth century. Clan Buchanan.

CORRIE. Territorial, from the lands of that name in Dumfries-shire, used as a surname since the twefth century. George Corrie emigrated to East New Jersey in 1685, and James Corry went to Virginia in 1698.

CORRIGIL, CORRIGALL. Territorial, from the lands of Corrigall in Orkney, used as a surname since the late fifteenth century. Derived from the Old Norse term *'karri-gil'* meaning 'valley of the cock-ptarmigan'. A few Corrigils from Orkney settled in Richmond County, Georgia, just before the American Revolution.

CORSAR, COSSAR. An Anglo-Saxon occupational surname meaning 'horse dealer'. John Corsar emigrated to New England by 1716, and William Cossar was a founder member of the Scots Charitable Society of Boston in 1657.

CORSTORHINE. Derived from the village of that name near Edinburgh. The placename is probably a corruption of *'Cross of Thorfinn'*.

Used as a surname since the sixteenth century. Robert Corstophine settled in Halifax County, North Carolina, before 1778.

COULL. Territorial, from a place of that name in Aberdeenshire, used as a surname since the thirteenth century. Possibly from the Gaelic word *'cuil'* meaning 'corner'. Reverend James Coull settled in Antigua in 1772, and John Coul was in Westmoreland County, Virginia, by 1654.

COULTER. Territorial, from Coulter in Lanarkshire, used as a surname since the thirteenth century. From the Gaelic *'cul tir'* meaning 'back land'. Hugh Coulter, a merchant, settled in Maryland before 1763, and John Couter, a tradesman, went to Hudson Bay in 1683.

COURTNEY. Territorial, brought from France to England and recorded in Scotland since the early modern period. Thomas Courtney, from Berwickshire, was in Boston by 1770.

COUTIE. Territorial, derived from the lands of the Abbey of Cupar Angus in Perthshire. Uncommon with a few examples dating from the seventeenth century. David Cowtie, a Jacobite, was transported to Antigua in 1747.

COUTTS, COATS. Territorial, from Cults in Aberdeenshire, used as a surname since the fourteenth century. Perhaps from the Gaelic *'coillte'* meaning 'woods'. Hercules Coutts, a merchant from Montrose, settled in Maryland before 1751, Patrick Coutts, a merchant from Aberdeen, emigrated to Virginia in 1747, Mary Coats emigrated from Belfast to Philadelphia in 1773. Coutts is a sept of the Farquharson Clan.

COVENTRY. Territorial, from Coventry in England, found in Scotland since the thirteenth century. Originally localised in central east Scotland. Anne Coventry, from Edinburgh, was transported to the colonies in 1743

COWAN. An abbreviated version of 'MacCowan' which itself is an shortened verion of the Gaelic name *'Macilchomhghain'*. A common name in Lowland Scotland. John Cowan, a Cromwellian transportee, landed in Boston in 1652, while William Cowan, a Jacobite, was deported to the Chesapeake in 1747. Clan Donald or Clan Colquhoun.

COWE. Possibly descriptive. Examples date from the fourteenth century. Alester Cowe was transported to Boston in 1652.

CRAICH, CREECH, CREICH. Territorial, derived from the lands of Creich in Fife. A Gaelic place name which has been used as a surname since around 1200. John Craich, a weaver from Peebles, emigrated to Darien in 1698.

CRAIG, CRAG. Craig means 'rock' in Gaelic, *'creag'*, and is, or is part of, many place names in Scotland. It is also relatively common in Ulster. One of the original Scottish undertakers of the Plantation of Ulster was a Sir James Craig. A number of Craigs settled in East New Jersey during the 1680s.

CRAIGHEAD. Territorial, derived from one of a number of places of that name. Examples date from the late fifteenth century. George Craighead was transported to America in 1750

CRAIGIE, CRAIGEN. A Gaelic descriptive surname indicating a place of residence – *'at the crag'*. John Craigen, was transported to Boston in 1651, and Hugh Craigie was in Boston by 1715.

CRANE. Probably an Old English personal name. The earliest example dates from the mid-thirteenth century. Peter Crane, a Jacobite from Perthshire, was transported to the American colonies in 1747.

CRANSTON. Territorial, derived from the barony of that name near Edinburgh. Cranston signifies the *'tun'* or settlement of *'Cran'*. A surname if Scotland since the thirteenth century. George Cranston died in the Bahamas in 1790.

CRAWFORD. Territorial, taken from the barony of Crawford in Lanarkshire, used as a surname since the twefth century. Patrick Crawford, was a merchant in New York, 1699, Reverend Thomas Crawford was in Delaware by 1709, and James Crawford emigrated from Larne to Charleston in 1773. The Crawfords are linked with the Lindsays.

CREIGHTON, CRICHTON, CRIGHTON. Territorial, from the barony of Crichton in Midlothian, used as a surname since the twefth century. Several Jacobites named Crichton or Crighton were transported to America during the eighteenth century.

CROCKER. Occupational, equivalent to 'potter'. A very rare surname in Scotland with examples since the sixteenth century. Robert Croaker was a seaman aboard the St Andrew on the voyage to Darien in 1698, and High Crocker, emigrated to Philadelphia in 1774.

CROCKETT. Found in central Scotland since the thirteenth century. A family of Crocketts from Coupar Angus in Perthshire, settled in South Carolina in the mid-eighteenth century.

CROMAR. Territorial, derived from Cromar in Aberdeenshire. James Cromar, a schoolmaster from Aberdeenshire, died in Virginia 1758.

CROMARTY. Territorial, derived from the burgh of Cromarty, or in Gaelic *'Crom-badh'* meaning 'crooked bay'. Most early examples of the surname come from Orkney and date from the sixteenth century. William Cromartie, from South Ronaldsay, settled in North Carolina in 1758.

CROMBIE. An Aberdeenshire name originating in a place of that name in Auchterless. William Crombie, a saddler from Elgin, settled in Boston before 1764. Crombie may be a sept of Clan Donald or of the Gordon Clan.

CROMERY. Possibly a variant of 'Comrie' and thus a territorial surname based on the name of a village in Perthshire. James and Patrick Cromery, from Breadalbane in Perthshire, emigrated to New York in 1775.

CROOKS. A surname introduced into Scotland as *'Croc'* during the twelfth century. Many of the early examples come from south west Scotland. James Crooks died in Darien in 1699, and John Crooks went to Hudson Bay in 1684.

CROOKSHANK, CRUICKSHANK. Probably descriptive. Early examples tend to come from north-east Scotland. Alexander Cruikshank, a merchant from Aberdeen, died in Antigua during 1713, while Elizabeth Cruickshank, from Aberdeen, was banished to Virginia in 1751.

CROSBIE, CORSEBY. From the Danish, or possibly Old English, word meaning 'the village with the cross'. James Corsebie, a Covenanter, was banished to Jamaica in 1685, and another Covenanter, David Crosbie, was transported to the West Indies in 1678.

CROSS. Descriptive, indicating a place of residence, at or near the cross. Reverend John Cross settled in Philadelphia during 1732, and John Cross, from Glasgow, died at Cape Fear, North Carolina, in 1773.

CRUDEN. Territorial, probably Gaelic, from the lands of Cruden in Aberdeenshire. Uncommon, the surname tended to be localised in north-east Scotland. Reverend Alexander Cruden, from Aberdeen, was the minister of South Farnham, Virginia, in the eighteenth century.

CULLEN. Territorial, from the town of Cullen in Banffshire. Possibly based on the Gaelic *cuilan'* meaning 'little nook'. Examples date from the medieval period. James Cullen, was clerk to the Council of Maryland in 1687, while David Cullens, emigrated to New York in 1775.

CUMIN, CUMMING. Believed to be derived from the town of Comines in France. It appears as a surname in Scotland during the twefth century. John Cumming died in Salem, Massachusetts, in 1663, and Alexander Cummin was a Jacobite transported to Virginia in 1716.

CUNNINGHAM. Territorial, from the district of Cunningham in north Ayrshire. The suffix *'ham'* suggests an English origin. Used as a surname since the thirteenth century. Arthur Cunningham was transported to South Carolina in 1684, Dr Henry Cunningham, from Edinburgh, died in St Augustine in 1771, and Lieutenant James Cunningham of the Royal North British Fusiliers, from County Antrim, died in Florida before 1769.

CUNNISON or MACCONICH. An uncommon surname found in late medieval Perthshire. William Cunnison, a millwright from Lanarkshire, settled in Jamaica before 1779.

CURRIE, CURRY. Either from a placename Currie in Midlothian or a place called Corrie in Dumfries-shire, alternatively an Anglicised version of the Gaelic names 'MacVurich' alias 'McMhuirich'. Early examples are found in southern Scotland and are thus likely to be of territorial origin, while those from the Gaelic options tend to come from Islay or Mull. William Curry was in Boston by 1695, while Walter Currie, from Linlithgow, settled in Rhode Island by 1739. Some Curries claim allegiance to the MacDonalds and others to the MacPhersons.

CUTHBERT. An old Anglo-Saxon name popularised in south-east Scotland and north east England by St Cuthbert of Lindisfarne. A branch of the family settled in Inverness during the fifteenth century and some of their descendents settled in Georgia from the 1730s, from where a branch settled in Jamaica after the American Revolution.

CUTHBERTSON. Patronymic, meaning 'son of Cuthbert'. Found in Scotland from the fifteenth century. William Cuthbertson, a Covenanter, was transported to Virginia in 1669

DALGETTY. Territorial, from the lands of Dalgety in Fife and from those in Aberdeenshire. The Gaelic prefix '*dail*' means 'field'. Relatively uncommon. Alexander and John Dalgetty, both Jacobites, were transported to America in 1716.

DALGLEISH. Territorial, from the lands of Dalgleish in Selkirkshire. It is a Gaelic name bearing the prefix '*dail*' or 'field' with, probably, the word '*gleois*' or 'activity'. Found as a surname initially on the Borders in the fifteenth century but later in Fife and Perthshire. An Alexander Dalgleish, a Covenanter, was transported to East New Jersey in 1685, while another of that name took part in the Darien Expedition of 1698.

DALLAS. Territorial, from the barony of that name in Morayshire. Used as a surname since the thirteenth century. Walter Dallas, a merchant from Edinburgh, settled in Annapolis, Maryland, before 1772, and Alexander Dallas, a merchant from Aberdeen, emigrated to Jamaica in 1775. Clan Macintosh.

DALMAHOY. Territorial, from the barony of Dalmahoy near Edinburgh. Relatively uncommon. Early recordings of the surname tend to come from the neighborhood of Edinburgh. Thomas Dalmahoy, a Jacobite, was transported to St Kitts in 1716.

DALRYMPLE. From the Gaelic '*dail chruim puill*' meaning 'field on the curving stream', a place in Ayrshire. Used as a surname since the fourteenth century. John Dalrymple, from Galloway, settled in North Carolina in 1775, and David Dalrymple went to St Kitts before 1774.

DALYELL, DALZIELL, DALZELL. Territorial, from the barony of that name in Lanarkshire. From Gaelic '*Dail-ghil*' the white field. First used as a surname in the thirteenth century. Reverend Dalziel from Edinburgh settled in Bermuda in 1779, and John Dalyell emigrated to Maryland before 1765.

DARLING. Probably an Old English surname. Found in south-east Scotland since the fourteenth century. John Darling, a cordwainer, emigrated to Maryland in 1684, while George Darling, was a prisoner of war, shipped by Oliver Cromwell to Boston in 1650.

DARRACH. A territorial name based on the Gaelic word for 'a man from Jura', although in some cases it may derive from a place name in Stirlingshire . Jenny Darrach from Jura, Argyll, settled in North Carolina in 1768. Clan Donald.

DAVIDSON, DAVIESON. Patronymic, in use as a surname in Scotland since the fourteenth century, at least. Common throughout Lowland Scotland. In the Highlands the family is known as '*clan daidh*', which is part of the Clan Chattan confederation. Several Jacobites bearing the surname Davidson were banished to America in 1716 and 1747. Reverend Alexander Davidson settled in Maryland during 1710, and John Davidson, from Aberdeen, was transported to Barbados by 1666. Clan Davidson.

DAVIE. Patronymic, a diminutive of David. Marion Davie was transported to the American colonies in 1766. Clans Davidson and Chattan.

DAWSON. Another surname derived from 'David'. William Dawson, from Perth, was a minister in West Florida before 1770. Clans Davidson and Chattan.

DEAN. Probably based on the Old English word *'dene'* meaning valley and found as a placename, or signifying a 'Dane'. Used as a surname in Scotland since the fourteenth century. John Dean, a minister, went to Carolina in 1723, while another John Dean, a Glasgow merchant, settled Tappahannaock, Virginia, by 1757.

DEAS. Possibly a variant of Dyce, a burgh in Aberdeenshire, thus a territorial surname. Based on a Gaelic word *'deis'* or *'deas'* meaning 'to the south'. Found as Deas in Angus and Edinburgh from the seventeenth century but as Diss or Dyes in Aberdeenshire from the fifteenth century. David Deas, a merchant, died in Charleston in 1775. Clan Skene.

DEMPSTER. Occupational, from the office of dempster (*doomster)* or judge. William Dempster, probably a Cromwellian deportee, was in Virginia by 1654, and Lily Dempster emigrated to Philadelphia in 1775..

DENHAM, DENHOLM. Territorial, derived from the barony of Denholm in Roxburghshire. Examples date from the late thirteenth century mostly from the Borders. Thomas Denham, settled in Charleston before 1776, later moved to Shelborne, Nova Scotia, while Elizabeth Denholm settled in Jamaica by 1753.

DENISTON, DENNISTOUN. Territorial, derived from the lands of Danielstoun in Renfrewshire. The surname appears as Danielstoun nuntil the sixteenth century when it becomes modified to Dennistoun or variant. Alison Deniston, from Edinburgh, was transported to Virginia in 1696, while Samuel Denniston emigrated from Kirkcudbright to New York in 1774.

DENNY. Territorial, originally the name of a town in Dunbartonshire but used as a surname since the fourteenth century. James Denny was in Boston by 1736.

DENOVAN. Territorial, based on Denovan in Stirlingshire, from the Gaelic *'dun aibhne'* meaning 'the fort by the river'. James Denovan, a horse thief, was banished to the American colonies in 1763.

DEUCHAR. Territorial, derived from the lands of Deuchar in Angus. Used as a surname since the medieval period but relatively rare. Alexander Deuchar, from Aberdeenshire, was a clergyman in Barbados during the early eighteenth century. Clan Lindsay.

DEWAR. Probably (1) a Gaelic descriptive name based on the word *'deoradh'* meaning pilgrim, (2) territorial, derived from the lands of Dewar in Midlothian. Used as a surname since the thirteenth century. Three men bearing the surname Dewar were members of the Scots Charitable Society of Boston in the seventeenth century. Clan MacNab.

DICK. Patronymic, a diminutive of Richard, used as a surname since the fifteenth century. Jean Dick was deported to the American Plantations in 1695, while John Dick, a Covenanter, was transported to Carolina in 1684.

DICKIE. Another diminutive of Richard. A surname found in Scotland since the sixteenth century. Nathaniel Dickie emigrated from Belfast to Philadelphia in 1773.

DICKMAN. Probably an occupational surname meaning 'ditcher'. James Dickman, a farmer from Perthshire, emigrated to Salem, New England, in 1775.

DICKSON, DIXON. Patronymic, meaning 'the son of Dick'. Used as a surname since the early fourteenth century, largely found on the Borders. Some Dickson families moved to Ulster in the early seventeenth century. Alexander Dickson, a soldier from Peebles-shire, settled in West Florida by 1774, and John Dickson was a member of the Scots Charitable Society of Boston in 1690.

DINGWALL. Territorial, derived from the land of Dingwall in Easter Ross. Possibly from Old Norse *'dinga voll r'* signifying 'meeting of the local council'. Daniel and Donald Dingwall were transported as Jacobite rebels to the West Indies. Clan Munro or Clan Ross.

DINWIDDIE, DUNWOODIE. Territorial, derived from the barony of Dinwoodie in Dumfries-shire. Possibly from *'din gwydd'*, British for 'the hill with the shrubs'. Used as a surname since around 1200. John Dinwiddie, from Glasgow, settled in Hanover, Virginia, by 1725

DISHINGTON. Territorial, derived from the lands of Dissington in Northumberland. Dissington comes from the Old English name *'Dicing a tun'* meaning the 'settlement of the family of Dica'. Most early examples of the surname in Scotland come from Fife but also Angus and Orkney, and date from the fourteenth century. John Dishington emigrated via Barbados to New York, arriving in 1689.

DOBIE, DOBBIE. A patronymic, an abbreviation of Robert, used throughout Lowland Scotland since the fifteenth century. James Dobie emigrated to East New Jersey in 1684.

DOCTOR. An uncommon surname of occupational origin. David Doctor, a Jacobite, was transported to South Carolina in 1716.

DOD, DODD, DODDS. Possibly from an Anglo-Saxon personal name, alternatively from the lands of Doddis in Berwickshire. James Dodds, a Jacobite from Haddington, was transported to Jamaica in 1747.

DOIG. A surname traditionally found in Stirlingshire, Perthshire and Angus. Charles Doig, from Perthshire, emigrated to Philadelphia in 1775, and James Doig, from Montrose, died in Antigua in 1759.

DONALD, DONNELL. A Gaelic name, *'domnhall'*, based on the biblical name *'Daniel'*. Some Highlanders, settling in a Lowland Scots community, chose to drop the prefic 'Mac' possibly to assimilate more quickly. Thus certain people bearing the name 'Donald' were actually MacDonalds several generations ago. David Donald or MacDonald, son of David MacDonald of Shangzie, perished at Darien in 1699, and Robert Donald, from Dunbartonshire, was a merchant in Virginia before 1757. Walter

Donnell was in Westmoreland County, Virginia, by 1654. Clan Donald.

DONALDSON. Patronymic, based on *'son of Donald'*, or possibly an Anglicised version of *'MacDonald'*. Examples date back to the thirteenth century. Also found in County Antrim and County Armagh. Several Jacobites called Donaldson were exiled to the Chesapeake in 1716 and 1747. Clan Donald.

DOUGALL. Descriptive, from the Gaelic *'dughall'* meaning the 'dark stranger' possibly the Norse Viking. Sometimes an abbreviation of MacDougall. Arthur Donaldson, a Covenanter from Glasgow, was banished to the West Indies in 1678, and Walter Dougall, from Paisley, emigrated to New York in 1774. Clan MacDougall.

DOUGLAS. From the Gaelic *'dhu glas'* meaning 'dark stream'. Examples of the surname date from the late twelfth century. A common surname in Scotland. James Douglas from Dunbartonshire, died in Dumfries, Virginia, in 1766, and Hugh Douglas emigrated to Virginia on the <u>Constance</u> in 1635. Clan Douglas.

DOULL. Patronymic, probably a corruption of the Gaelic name *'domnhall'*, or Donnell. James Doull, a surgeon from Edinburgh, settled in Maryland before 1751. Possibly Clan Donald.

DOW. Descriptive, derived from the Gaelic word for 'black' – *'dubh'*. A surname recorded since the sixteenth century. John Dow, a Jacobite from Perthshire, was exiled to Maryland in 1747. Clan Chattan.

DOWIE. Possibly an abbreviation of *'Macildowie'* meaning 'son of the dark servant'. William Dowie, a clergyman, was despatched to Maryland in 1762.

DOWNIE. Territorial, derived from the barony of Downie near Dundee. Possibly Gaelic if it bears the prefix *'dun'* meaning 'fort'. Examples date back to the thirteenth century. Katherine and Christian Downie, from Glen Orchy, emigrated to North Carolina in 1775.

DRENAN. A rare name found in Galloway. William Drennan, a Covenanter, was transported to Jamaica in 1685.

DREVER, DRIVER. A surname traditionally found in Orkney and Shetland, dating from the fifteenth century. James Driver was indentured in Chester County, Pennsylvania, during 1693.

DRUMMOND. Territorial, taken from the barony of Drymen in Stirlingshire. Possibly based on the Gaelic word *'dromainn'* meaning 'a ridge'. Used as a surname since the late twelfth century.

William Drummond participated in Bacon's Rebellion in Virginia, and was subsequently executed, and John Drummond, a cooper, emigrated to North Carolina in 1775. Clan Drummond.

DRYDEN. Territorial, derived from one of two places in south east Scotland, and used as a surname since the late thirteenth century. The name is English meaning *'dry valley'*. Adam Dryden, emigrated to Georgia in 1774.

DRYSDALE. Territorial, from Dryfesdale in Dumfries-shire, and signifying *'the valley of the river Dryfe'*. Recorded as a surname in Scotland since the fifteenth century. John Drysdale, a Covenanter, was exiled to the West Indies in 1681.

DUFF. A name of Gaelic origin containing the prefix *'dubh'* meaning 'dark'. A surname used since the late thirteenth century. A number of Duffs were banished as Jacobites to the American colonies after the Risings of 1715 and 1745. Clan MacDuff.

DUFFUS. Territorial, from the lands of Duffus in Morayshire. A surname in Scotland since the thirteenth century. Most early examples tend to be localised in north east Scotland. Daniel Duffus, a Jacobite, was transported to Antigua in 1716. Clan Sutherland.

DUFFY. An Anglicisation of the Gaelic name *'Dhuibhshith'* meaning ' the dark peaceful one'. Duncan Duffie, from Edinburgh, settled in New York before 1763. Clan MacFee.

DUGDALE. Probably territorial from Dugdale in England, or possibly a variant of Dugall. William Dugdale settled in New York by 1715.

DUN, DUNN. Either descriptive from the word *'dunn'* meaning brown, or territorial, from Dun in Angus, or possibly from the Gaelic word meaning 'hill-fort'. The surname has been recorded since the thirteenth century. John and Alexander Dunn, possibly from Montrose, were indentured servants who settled in East New Jersey in 1684.

DUNBAR. Territorial, from the barony of Dunbar in East Lothian. Dunbar is a Gaelic word containing *'dun'* or 'fort' and *'barr'* or 'height', thus the 'fort on the height'. A surname in use since the thirteenth century. Three Jacobite Dunbars were exiled to the American colonies during the eighteenth century, and George Dunbar was one of the early settlers of Georgia. Clan Dunbar.

DUNCAN. While the origin of the name is unclear it is likely to be Gaelic. The prefix *'dun'* can mean 'hill-fort', while *'ceann'* is 'head'. Examples exist back to the medieval period. James Duncan was a shipmaster in late seventeenth century New York, while John Duncan arrived in Pennsylvania in 1697, and James Duncan emigrated from Belfast to Philadelphia in 1771. Clan Donnachaidh alias Robertson.

DUNDAS. Territorial, from Dundas in West Lothian. Possibly derived from the Gaelic *'dun deas'* meaning 'south-hill'. Examples date from the early thirteenth century. Not too common. John Dundas was the master of the <u>Warwick</u> trading from London to Virginia in 1631, and James Dundas was a Covenanter who was banished to East New Jersey in 1685.

DUNDEE. Territorial, derived from the burgh of Dundee. Possibly based on the Gaelic words *'dun De'* meaning 'fort of the Tay'. Used as a surname in Scotland from the thirteenth century and in Ulster from the seventeenth. Found in Pennsylvania among the Scotch-Irish during the eighteenth century. David Dundee, a Scots indentured servant, absconded in South Carolina in 1744.

DUNLOP. Territorial, taken from the lands of Dunlop in north Ayrshire. Probably from the Gaelic *'dun lapach'* meaning 'muddy hill'. Used as a surname since the thirteenth century. Taken to Ulster by settlers during the seventeenth century. John Dunlap from Strabane founded the *Pennsylvania Packet* in 1771. Reverend William Dunlop was one of the leaders of the Scots settlers in Stuartstown, South Carolina, in 1684.

DUNMORE, DUNSMUIR, DINSMORE. Territorial, taken from the lands of Dundemore in north Fife. Possibly from the Gaelic meaning *'the great fort"*. Used as a surname in Scotland since the thirteenth century and in Ulster since the early seventeenth century. John and Mary Dunmore, from Glasgow, emigrated to Salem in 1775.

DURHAM, Territorial, from the town in north-east England. Recorded in Scotland since the thirteenth century especially in Angus. Mary Durham emigrated to Baltimore in 1775.

DURIE, DURY. Territorial, derived from the lands of Durie near Kirkcaldy. Based on the Gaelic word *'dobharach'* meaning 'a watery place'. Examples date from the thirteenth century. Isobel Dury, a Covenanter, was transported to East New Jersey in 1685.

DURRAR. A surname of unknown origin. William Durrar, a Jacobite from Aberdeen, was transported to the American colonies in 1747.

DUYS. Probably based on a Gaelic name. Donald McWilliam Duys was deported to the American colonies in 1752.

DYER. Occupational, probably English as in Scotland the title 'Litster' was more commonly used. Rare in Scotland. Mary Dyer, a vagrant, was transported to the colonies in 1751.

DYKES. Territorial, taken from the lands of Dykes in the barony of Strathaven. Possibly originating in the Old English word *'dyke'*, meaning ditch. Andrew Dykes, a Covenanter, was banished to the American Plantations in 1684.

DYSART. Territorial, from Gaelic *'diseart'* originally a deserted site later the place of a hermit, as in Dysart, Fife. Relatively uncommon, with a few examples dating from the late medieval period. George Dysart, a Jacobite, was transported to South Carolina in 1716

EASTON. Old English, perhaps *'east –tun'* meaning 'east settlement', derived from places of that name in southern Scotland. Examples date from the late thirteenth century. Thomas Easton, a baker from Edinburgh, emigrated to Maryland in 1719.

ECCLES. Territorial, from places of that name based on the Gaelic word *'eaglais'* meaning 'church'. Used as a surname since the late twefth century. William Eccles emigrated from Stranraer to North Carolina in 1775.

EDGAR. An Old English personal name made popular in Scotland by King Edgar who reigned from 1097 to 1107. The early examples of the surname tend to come from Berwickshire, Dumfries and Galloway. In Ulster the name became Eggar or Eager. John Edgar, from Dumfries, was a member of the Scots Charitable Society of Boston in 1694.

EDINBURGH. Territorial, from Old English, meaning *'Edwin's burgh'*. Rare, only a few examples in Scottish historical documents. John Edenburgh was among the Scots colonists in South Carolina in 1685.

EDMONSTONE. Territorial, from the Anglian, meaning the *'tun'* or settlement of *'Edmond'*, in Midlothian, Berwickshire and Lanarkshire. Examples date from around 1200 in southern Scotland and from the mid sixteenth century in the Shetland Islands. William Edmonstone, from Stirling, settled in Jamaica before 1774.

EDWARD. An Old English personal name used in Scotland as a surname since the mid-fifteenth century. Two Covenanters bearing the surname were transported to Carolina in 1684.

EGGOE. A rare Gaelic surname found in north-east Scotland since the late medieval period. John and William Eggoe, Jacobite rebels, were transported to South Carolina in 1716.

EGLINTON. Territorial, from the lands of Eglinton in north Ayrshire. An Anglian term, signifying the *'tun'* or settlement of *'Eglin'*. Relatively uncommon, examples date from the early thirteenth century. William Eglinton, a rioter in Glasgow, was banished to the American colonies in 1751.

ELDER. Presumably descriptive. Used as a surname since the fifteenth century. Reverend John Elder settled in Pennsylvania during 1736, and another John Elder, a smith from Glasgow, emigrated to New York in 1775. Some Elders belong to the Clan Macintosh.

ELGIN. Territorial, from the town of Elgin in Morayshire. A rare surname. The earliest example of the surname dates from the early thirteenth century. James Elgin emigrated to Virginia in 1774.

ELLICE. Possibly a variation of the biblical name *Elias*. Examples of the name exist from the early sixteenth century in Scotland and in Ulster from the seventeenth century. George Ellice died in Philadelphia by 1753.

ELLIOT. Possibly of Anglian origin. A long established surname on the Borders, examples date back to the medieval period. Found in Ulster since the early seventeenth century. Charles Elliot, the Attorney General of North Carolina, died there in 1756, John Elliot, Governor of West Florida, died in 1769, and James Elliot, from Ireland to Philadelphia by 1769.

EMIRY. Possibly a Walloon surname. James Emiry, a weaver, emigrated to New York in 1774.

ENGLISH. (see Inglis, below). James English was transported to New England in 1651

ERBURY. A territorial surname of unknown origin. Harry Erbury, from Orkney, was apprenticed aboard a New England ship in 1711.

ERSKINE. Territorial, from the barony of Erskine in Renfrewshire. Used as a surname since 1225. Henry Erskine, Lord Cardross, brought a group of Scottish settlers to Stuartstown, South Carolina, in 1684, and George Erskine, a minister, settled in Jamaica in 1711.

ESPLIN. Probably a corruption of the biblical name *Absolom*. Found in east central Scotland from the sixteenth century. John Esplin, a soldier, died in Darien on 1 July 1700.

EUNSON. An Orcadian version of Ewanson, found in the islands since the seventeenth century. George Eunson, from Kirkwall, settled in Richmond County, Georgia, in 1774.

EWAN, EWING. From the Gaelic personal name *Eoghann*. Examples date from the sixteenth century. George Ewing, from Edinburgh, emigrated to Dominica in 1774. A sept of the Clan MacLachlan.

EWART. Territorial, from a place in Northumberland. Examples date from the sixteenth century and tend to come from the Borders. Jean Ewart was transported to Maryland in 1771.

FAA, FAW. A surname found among the gypsies on the Borders. In 1671 a number of them were ordered to be captured and transported to Virginia, later in 1715 a couple of different Faas was transported there.

FAIRBAIRN. Probably a descriptive surname but possibly a variant of 'Freebairn' (see below). Examples date from the fourteenth century. John Fairbairn, a Covenanter, was banished to the West Indies in 1678.

FAIRHOLM. Territorial, from the lands of Fairholm, later Farme, in Lanarkshire. Examples date from the seventeenth century. Thomas Fairholm settled in Tobago before 1783.

FAIRLIE. Territorial, derived from the lands of Fairlie in Ayrshire. James Fairlie was a merchant in New York and Virginia before the American Revolution and thereafter in Jamaica.

FAIRWEATHER. A surname found in Scotland since the fifteenth century especially around Dundee. Robert Fairweather, a barber from Dundee, died in Charleston in 1763.

FALA. Territorial, taken from the lands of Fala in Midlothian. Used as a surname since the twelfth century. John Fala, a Covenanter from Kelso, was banished to the American Plantations in 1684.

FALCONER. Occupational, meaning one who breeds or trains falcons. The surname was recorded from the thirteenth century with some degree of localisation in the north-east. Reverend James Falconer settled in York, Virginia, in 1718, and Patrick Falconer emigrated to East New Jersey in 1684.

FARNELL. Territorial, taken from the lands of Farnell in Angus. It dates from the early thirteenth century as a surname. Mary Farnell was in Gloucester County, Virginia, by 1655.

FARQUHAR. From the Gaelic personal name *'fearchar'*. In early medieval documents it appears as a forename but by the fourteenth century it was an established surname. William Farquhar, settled in Maryland during the early eighteenth century, and Alexander Farquhar emigrated to Pennsylvania in 1728. Clan Farquharson.

FARQUHARSON. Meaning 'Son of Farquhar', the family dates from the mid fourteenth century. Traditionally localised in Upper Deeside, Aberdeenshire. A number of Farquharsons were exiled to the American colonies in 1716 and in 1747 for their allegiance to the Jacobite cause. Clan Farquharson.

FARRIES. A surname found in Dumfries and Galloway since the seventeenth century. William Fairies emigrated from Larne to Charleston in 1773.

FENTON. Territorial, originating in the barony of Fenton in East Lothian. Possibly from Old English meaning the *'settlement or tun in the fens'*. Most of the early recordings of the name originate between Angus and the Lothians. Alexander Fenton, a surgeon from Dundee, emigrated to Antigua in 1738, while Richard Fenton settled in Georgia in 1774.

FENWICK. Territorial, taken from the parish of Fenwick in Ayrshire. Possibly from Old English meaning *'the farm in the marshes'*. James Fenwick was transported to East New Jersey in 1685.

FERGUS. From the Gaelic forename *'fearghus'*. A very rare surname. James Fergus, a Glasgow weaver, emigrated to New York in 1774. Clan Ferguson.

FERGUSON. Patronymic, partly Gaelic with the English suffix 'son'. A surname since the fifteenth century, found in various parts of Scotland but especially in Aberdeenshire, Perthshire and Ayrshire. Many of the Fergusons of Colonial America arrived in chains, some as Cromwellian transportees, a few as banished Covenanters, and others as Jacobite exiles. Clan Ferguson.

FIDDES. Territorial, derived from the barony of Fiddes in Kincardineshire. Examples of it and variants date from the thirteenth century. David Fiddes, a Jacobite from Angus, was transported to Barbados in 1747.

FIELD. A descriptive surname, indicating a place of residence, of English origin. James Field arrived in York County, Virginia, during 1666.

FIFE, FYFFE. Territorial, from the county of Fife, one of the old Pictish kingdoms. Used as a surname since the thirteenth century. Duncan Phyfe settled in New York in 1783, and James Fife settled in Charleston, South Carolina, in 1774.

FIMISTER, PHEEMISTER. Occupational, from the Old English word *'feoh'* meaning 'cattle' and the word 'master', that is a man in charge of a herd of cattle. A surname found in north east Scotland. A group of Fimisters emigrated to Philadelphia in 1775.

FINDLATER, FINLATOR. Territorial, taken from the lands of Findlater in Banffshire. Derived from the Gaelic *'fionn leitir'* meaning 'white hillside'. Not a common surname, with examples localised in north east Scotland. Reverend John Findlater went to the West Indies in 1771.

FINDLAY, FINLAY. From the Gaelic *'fionn lagh'*, meaning 'fair' or 'white hero'. Originally a forename later adopted as a surname, used as the latter since the sixteenth century. John Finlay was a member of the Scots Charitable Society of Boston in 1687, and Robert Finlay, from Glasgow, settled in Maryland before 1772. Clan Farquharson.

FINDLAYSON, FINLAYSON. A hybrid surname, partly Gaelic and partly English, with early examples coming from central and north east Scotland since the thirteenth century. Finlay Finlayson, from Ross-shire, was banished to the American colonies in 1751. Clan Farquharson.

FINNELSTONE. Territorial, probably derived from the lands of Finnieston in Glasgow. John Finnelston, from Paisley, settled in Philadelphia in 1774.

FINNEY, FINNIE. A Gaelic name bearing the prefix 'fin' or *'fionn'* meaning 'white' or 'fair'. A surname in use since the sixteenth century. Reverend Alexander Finnie emigrated to Virginia in 1724, and Reverend William Finney emigrated there by 1714.

FINNISON. Patronymic, signifying 'son of Finnie'. Peter Finnison and John Finnison, both Covenanters, were banished to the colonies in the 1689s.

FISHER. An English surname of occupational origin which has been used in Scotland since the fourteenth century. A group of Fishers, from Breadalbane in Perthshire, emigrated to New York in 1775.

FITCHETT. The etymology of this name is unclear. It may be based on a place name, as yet unidentified, or possibly it a Norman French surname bearing the prefix '*fitz*'. The early examples tend to come from eastern Scotland. James Fitchett, probably from Montrose, emigrated to East New Jersey in 1684.

FLEMING. Territorial, indicating a native of Flanders. During the medieval period there was small scale Flemish immigration into Scotland, a number settled in Lanarkshire while individual merchants and craftsmen could be found in east coast burghs. Examples date from the twelfth century. Patrick Fleming, from Kirkintilloch, was in Accomack County, Virginia, by 1663, John Fleming, a Covenanter from Stirlingshire, was transported to Carolina in 1684, and Alexander Fleming emigrated from Larne to Charleston in 1773. Some Flemings are affiliated to the Clan Murray.

FLETCHER. Occupational, taken from the Old French term '*flechier*' meaning 'arrow maker'. Sometimes confused with the surname Flesher, based on the old term for a butcher. Used in Scotland since the fourteenth century. John Fletcher died in Darien during 1698, Angus Fletcher, and his family, from Glen Orchy settled in North Carolina in 1774, and Thomas Fletcher emigrated from Ireland to Nova Scotia by 1761. Some Fletchers are affiliated to Clan McGregor.

FLETT. A surname from the Orkney Islands, possibly of Norse origin. Examples there date from the fifteenth century. Elizabeth Flett, from Orkney, settled in New England before 1772, and Robert Flatt arrived in Pennsylvania in 1695.

FLINT. Origin unknown. A very rare surname in Scotland. Earliest known example dates from the seventeenth century. James Flint, a Jacobite, was transported to South Carolina in 1716.

FOGO, FOGGO. Territorial, derived from the lands of Fogo in Berwickshire. Uncommon but examples date from the twelfth century. David Fogo was a merchant in Antigua by 1749 and James Fogo was a merchant in Jamaica by 1771.

FORBES. Territorial, derived from the lands of Forbes in Aberdeenshire. Used as a surname since the thirteenth century, especially in north east Scotland. John Forbes, from Aberdeenshire, settled in East New Jersey in 1684, and Reverend John Forbes emigrated to St Augustine, East Florida, in 1764. Clan Forbes.

FORD, FOORD. Locational, from residing by a ford. Examples date from the fifteenth century. John Ford, a Covenanter, was transported to East New Jersey in 1685.

FORDYCE. Territorial, taken from the lands of Fordyce in Banffshire. Possibly from the Gaelic words *'fothir'* or 'field', and *'deas'* or 'south'. Used as a surname since the fifteenth century. Reverend John Fordyce died in Prince Frederick County, South Carolina, in 1751. Clan Forbes.

FORFAR. Territorial, from the burgh of Forfar in Angus. A surname since the late twelfth century. Relatively uncommon. Margaret Forfar, from Perthshire, emigrated to Philadelphia in 1775.

FORMAN, FOREMAN, FORMOND. Two derivations, one, territorial, from the land of Formond in Fife, the other, occupational, from 'foreman'. Examples of the names can be found as early as the thirteenth century. John Forman, a Covenanter, was transported to East New Jersey in 1684.

FORREST. Locational, from residing in or near a forest. A surname since the fourteenth century. James Forrest, a Covenanter, was transported to Jamaica in 1685 and Margaret Forrest, another Covenanter, to East New Jersey in 1685. Some Forrests belong to Clan Donald.

FORRESTER, FORSTER, FOSTER. Occupational, from the post of forest-keeper. In Scotland the surname has been recorded since the twelfth century. Members of a family of Border reivers named Forster moved to Ulster in the early seventeenth century. Andrew Forrester, from Dundee, was one of the leaders of the Scots settlers in Nova Scotia during the 1620s and 1630s.

FORRET. Territorial, from the lands of Forret in Fife. Most examples come from Fife and begin in the thirteenth century. James Forret in Rhode Island during 1637, was the agent for Sir William Alexander.

FORSYTH. Probably a name of territorial origin, possibly from Fauside. A surname in Scotland since the fourteenth century. Found also in Counties Antrim and Down since the Plantation of Ulster. Bezabeer

Forsyth emigrated to Carolina in 1774, while John Forsyth, from County Londonderry, emigrated to Pennsylvania in 1771.

FORTUNE. Territorial, derived from the lands of Fortune in East Lothian. Possibly bearing the Scandinavian suffix *'tun'* meaning 'settlement'. The surname dates from around 1200. William Fortune, a saddler from Edinburgh, emigrated to New York in 1775.

FOTHERINGHAM. Territorial, from Fotheringham in Angus. Recorded in various parts of Scotland since the thirteenth century. John Fotheringham, a Jacobite, was transported to South Carolina in 1716, and Reverend William Fotheringham died in Newfoundland in 1763.

FOULIS, FOWLIS. Territorial, from one of a number of places in Scotland. Examples date back to the thirteenth century. Reverend James Foulis emigrated to Virginia in 1750, and James Fowlles was a member of the Scots Charitable Society of Boston in 1684. Affiliated to Clan Munro.

FRASER, FRAZER. Derived from the Norman French *de Friselle* or *de Freseliere* and introduced into Scotland during the twefth century, gradually becoming Fraser or Frissell. A number of Jacobite Frasers were transported to South Carolina in 1716 also to Jamaica and Barbados in 1747. Clan Fraser.

FREEBAIRN. A surname dating from the twelfth century with most early examples originating from south east Scotland. James Freebairn, a physician, settled in Jamaica before 1769.

FREEMAN. A descriptive surname recorded in Scotland since the thirteenth century. James Freeman, from Aberdeen, settled in Maryland in 1730.

FRENCH. Descriptive, indicating the bearer's origin in France. Found in southern Scotland from the thirteenth century. Andrew and William French, both Covenanters, were transported to Barbados in 1685, and Patrick French, a Scotch-Irishman, was in Boston by 1716.

FREW. Territorial, from the lands of Frew in Perthshire. An uncommon surname dating from the sixteenth century. John Frew emigrated to Jamaica in 1773.

FRIGG. An unusual surname found in Morayshire. Andrew Frigg, a skipper from Findhorn, settled in Jamaica during the mid eighteenth century.

FRISSELL, FRIZELL. See 'Fraser' above. Found as a distinct surname in Scotland since the fifteenth century. Edward and George Frissell were Cromwellian transportees landed in Boston in 1652. Clan Fraser.

FROST. Probably a Huguenot surname introduced into Scotland in the seventeenth century. Robert, Thomas and William Frost arrived in East New Jersey in 1684.

FROUD. Territorial, from the lands of Frude in Peebleshire. Examples date from the sixteenth century. John Froud, from Nirthsdale, emigrated to Maryland in 1722, and James Fruid died there before 1725.

FULLAR, FOWLER. Occupational, either from *'fuller'* a 'waulker' or textile worker, or from *'fowler'* a poultryman. Examples date from the fourteenth century. John Fowler was transported to Virginia in 1775

FULLERTON. Territorial, from the barony of Fullerton in Ayrshire or Fullerton in Angus. Used as a surname since the thirteenth century. Robert Fullerton emigrated from Montrose to East New Jersey in 1684, and George Fullarton, a merchant from Ayrshire, died in Charleston before 1709.

FULTON. Territorial, possibly an abbreviation of *'Fullarton'*. Examples date from the thirteenth century. William Fulton settled in Bristol, New England, in the 1690s, and James Fulton emigrated to New York in 1774.

GADDIE, GEDDIE. A surname of Old English origin found on the east coast of Scotland since the fourteenth century. George Gaddie, from Aberdeenshire, was transported to the American colonies in 1752.

GAIR, GAYRE, GEAR. Either a territorial origin derived from the manor of Gayre in Cornwall or descriptive from the Gaelic word *'gearr'* meaning 'short'. Examples date back to at least the sixteenth century. John Gear, from Inverness, was in Boston by 1745. Clan Gayre.

GAIRDNER, GARDNER, GARDINER. An occupational surname recorded since the fifteenth century. John Gairdner, a Covenanter, was transported to New York in 1684, and Martin Gardner emigrated to Barbados in 1683.

GAIRNS. Probably a variant of Cairns (see above). John Gairns, a
carpenter from Dundee, emigrated to Cape Fear, North Carolina, in
1752.

GALBRAITH. From the Gaelic *'gille Breatnaich'* meaning 'servant of
the Briton'. The surname dates from the fourteenth century. Angus
Galbreath and his wife emigrated from Glen Orchy to North
Carolina in 1774, and James Galbraith, a baker from Glasgow,
settled in Quebec before 1773. A sept of Clan Donald.

GALL, GALT, GAUL. From the Gaelic word *'gall'* meaning a
'stranger'. Roger Gall was a merchant at the Bay of Honduras
around 1773, and Alexander Gall was transported to Virginia in
1755. A sept of Clan Donald.

GALLOWAY. Territorial, from the district of Galloway in south west
Scotland, and derived from the Gaelic *'Gall Gaidhel'* or 'strangers
Gaels'. It was used as a surname by the thirteenth century.
Christine Galloway was transported from Aberdeen to Virginia in
1668, Andrew Galloway was in East New Jersey by 1683, and
Andrew Galloway emigrated from Antrim to Philadelphia in 1774.

GAMBELL, GAMBLE. Probably a variant of Gammell a name of Norse
origin meaning 'old'. Initially a forename but by the fourteenth
century it was a surname, and by the seventeenth century it appeared
in Ulster. Adam Gambell, from Glasgow, died in North Carolina
before 1709.

GARDEN, GARDYNE. Territorial, from the barony of Gardyne in
Angus. The earliest example dates from 1296. Reverend Alexander
Garden settled in Charleston in 1719, and Dr Francis Garden died
there in 1770.

GARDNER, GARDINER. Occupational, derived from the occupation of
the same name. A surname in Scotland since the fifteenth century.
Patrick Gardner, a Jacobite, was transported to South Carolina In
1716, and William Gardner emigrated to Philadelphia in 1774.

GARGE. Possibly a variant of George. William Garge, from Orkney,
settled in Barbados before 1683.

GARLAND. Probably based on an Old English placename as yet
unidentified. In Scotland recordings of the surname date from the
thirteenth century. George Garland, a Glasgow barber, emigrated to
New York in 1775.

GARNOCK. From the Gaelic word *'carnach'* meaning a rocky place. A very unusual surname. George Garnock was banished to the colonies in 1768, and Duncan Garnoch indented in Edinburgh for 4 years service in East New Jersey in 1684.

GARSON. Patronymic, from the Old Norse *'Geirr –son'* meaning 'son of Geirr, or Gar'. Robert Garson, from Orkney, settled in Georgia in 1775.

GAULDIE, GALDIE, GOLDIE. Possibly descriptive, early examples come from Ayrshire and Lanarkshire. James Goldie, a ships carpenter from Ayrshire, emigrated to Quebec in 1775, and George Gauldie was transported from Aberdeen to Virginia in 1752.

GAULEY. Probably a contraction of *'MacAulay'*. Jean Gauley, from Ayrshire, emigrated to New York in 1774.

GAVIN. Patronymic, a Scots version of Gawain. Examples date from the seventeenth century. James and John Gavin were transported to Jamaica in 1685.

GAY. A descriptive surname dating back to the mid fifteenth century. Edward Gay, a Covenanter from Glasgow, was transported to the West Indies in 1678 and William Gay, a merchant, settled in Virginia by 1772.

GED, GEDD. A surname traditionally found in west Fife from the late thirteenth century. James and William Gedd, from Edinburgh, settled in Jamaica during the mid eighteenth century.

GEDDES. Territorial, from the lands of Geddes in Nairnshire. Examples of the surname date from the early fifteenth century. John Geddes emigrated to East New Jersey in 1684 and John Geddes, from Morayshire, settled in Georgia in 1737.

GEDDIE. A surname possibly of Anglo-Saxon origin found on the east coast of Scotland since the fourteenth century. James Donald Geddie, a farmer and cooper, settled in North Carolina in 1772.

GEEKIE, GEIKIE, GEGIE. Territorial, from the lands of Gagie in Angus. Most early examples of the name are found in Angus. Daniel Geekie, a surgeon, died in South Carolina before 1740.

GEILLS, GEILS. Possibly a variant of Giles. An uncommon surname. Andrew Geills was a merchant in Virginia by 1744.

GELLATLY. A local surname found in the vicinity of Dundee since the thirteenth century. Reverend Alexander Gellatly, from Perth, died in Warwick, Pennsylvania, in 1761.

GELLIBRAND, GILLIBRAND. An uncommon surname found in Scotland since the fourteenth century mostly in the north east. Reverend Andrew Gellibrand emigrated to New York in 1690.

GEMMILL, GAMMEL. Possibly from the Scandinavian *'gamle'* meaning 'old'. A forename in the twelfth century and a surname by the Fifteenth century. A standard surname in Ayrshire and Renfrewshire. Grissell Gemmill, a Covenanter, was transported to East New Jersey in 1685, and David Gammel drowned off Staten Island in 1763.

GENTLE. A descriptive surname of English origin which was used in Scotland since the seventeenth century. Robert Gentle, from Crieff, emigrated to Jamaica in 1750.

GENTLEMAN. An uncommon surname of unclear origin which has been found in Scotland since the fifteenth century. Margaret Gentleman emigrated from Montrose to East New Jersey in 1684.

GEORGE. Patronymic, an uncommon surname in Scotland although recordings of the name date back to the fifteenth century. James George, from the Shetland Islands, emigrated to Antigua in 1774.

GIBB, GIBBON. Diminutives of Gilbert. A relatively common surname found in Scotland since the sixteenth century. Alexander Gibb, from Linlithgow, settled in Maryland in 1730, and Dr William Gibbs was admitted to the Scots Charitable Society of Boston in 1693. Some people bearing these surnames claim allegiance to the Clan Buchanan while others to the Clan Campbell.

GIBSON. Patronymic, 'son of Gib', a standard Lowland Scottish surname dating from the fourteenth century. James Gibson, a merchant from Glasgow, was in Accomack County, Virginia, by 1731, and Colin Gibson, a tailor from Paisley, emigrated to New York in 1774. Some Gibsons identify with Clan Campbell and others with Clan Buchanan.

GIFFARD. A surname of Norman-French origin introduced to Scotland in the twelfth century. Early recordings of the name tend to come from East Lothian. John Giffard, a graduate of Edinburgh University, settled in the Leeward Islands in 1703.

GILBERT. Probably from on Old English personal name meaning *'bright hostage'* but possibly a variant of Gilbraith a surname based on the Gaelic meaning *'servant of the Briton'*. The surname has been recorded in Scotland since the thirteenth century. Ann Gilbert emigrated to South Carolina in 1767.

GILCHRIST. A descriptive surname of Gaelic origin. The surname is based on the words *'gille Criosd'* meaning 'the servant of Christ'. A surname since the thirteenth century. Angus Gilchrist, from Kintyre, settled in North Carolina in 1774, and Robert Gilchrist, a merchant from Berwickshire, died in Barbados in 1649. Gilchrists may be part of Clan Ogilvie.

GILFILLAN. Another such Gaelic surname – *'gille Fhaolin'*, meaning 'servant of (Saint) Fillan'. Used as a surname since the fourteenth century. John Gilfillan, a Covenanter, was banished to East New Jersey in 1685. Clan MacNab.

GILHAGIE. A very rare surname found in Ayrshire. Possibly bearing the Gaelic prefix *'gille'* – 'servant'. Ninian Gilhagie, sailed from Ayr bound for the West Indies in 1681.

GILKERSON. Possibly a variant of 'Gilgerston' a surname of territorial origin based on a placename in Perthshire. Gavin Gilkerson, a Covenanter, was transported to New York in 1684.

GILLESPIE. Descriptive, from the Gaelic *'gille easbuig'* meaning 'servant of the bishop'. Reverend George Gillespie, from Glasgow, died in Delaware in 1760, and another George Gillespie, a merchant from Dumfries, died in Maryland before 1724. Gillespie is associated with the Clan McPherson.

GILLIES, GILLIS. From the Gaelic *'gille Iosa'* meaning 'servant of Jesus'. McLaurin Gillies, from Glasgow, settled in Jamaica after 1766, and Thomas Gilliss was in Maryland by 1668.

GILLILAND, GILLAN. From the Gaelic surname *'Mac Gill Fhaolain'* meaning 'son of the servant of Fillan'. Found in Scotland and in Ulster. John Gilliland was transported to East New Jersey in 1685. Associated with the Clan McPherson.

GILMOUR, GILMORE. From the Gaelic *'gille Moire'* meaning 'servant of Mary' or perhaps from *'gille mhor'* signifying 'the great servant'. Initially used as a forename but by the early modern period it had become a surname. Archibald Gilmour was one of the partners of the Scottish Carolina Company in the 1680s, Robert

Gilmour was a merchant from Ayrshire who settled in Virginia by 1779, and David Gilmore emigrated from Ireland to Philadelphia in 1772. Clan Morrison.

GIRVAN. Territorial, from Girvan in Ayrshire. Possibly from the Gaelic *gear abhainn'* or 'the short river'. Scottish examples dates from the sixteenth century. Catherine Girvan was transported to East New Jersey in 1685, and John Girvan emigrated from Belfast to Philadelphia in 1773.

GIVEN. Territorial, probably from Govan in Lanarkshire but possibly from Giffen in Ayrshire. Examples of both date from the thirteenth century. John Given was a distiller in Boston in 1684, and Christine Govan, wife of James Grindlay, settled in Charleston before 1777.

GLASFORD, GLASSFORD. Territorial, from the lands of Glasford in Lanarkshire. James Glassford, a merchant from Glasgow, was in Quebec and later Boston and Norfolk, Virginia, before the American Revolution.

GLASGOW. Territorial, from the burgh of Glasgow. A surname used since the thirteenth century. Found also in Ulster. Reverend John Glasgow settled in Antigua in 1707, and Robert Glasgow, a surgeon, settled in St Vincent by 1777.

GLASS. Descriptive, from the Gaelic word *'glas'* for 'grey'. Examples date from the sixteenth century. Duncan Glass was in Norfolk, Virginia, by 1652, and William Glass emigrated from Stornaway to Philadelphia in 1774.

GLEN. Territorial, from the lands of Glen in Peebles-shire, derived from the Gaelic word *'gleann'* meaning 'valley'. Reverend William Glen settled in Maryland during 1707, and Walter Glen was in Boston by 1771. Some Glens are allied to the Clan MacPherson.

GLENCROSS. Territorial, from Glencrosh in Dumfries-shire, or from Glencorse, Midlothian.. Examples of this surname date from the fifteenth century. William Glencross was a merchant in New York before 1713.

GLENDINNING. Territorial, from the lands of Glendinning in Dumfries-shire and dating from the thirteenth century. They were one of the riding clans of the Scottish Borders some of whom took refuge in Ulster in the seventeenth century. Agnes Glendinning, from Edinburgh, was transported to Barbados in 1663

GLESSEN. Possibly a diminutive of MacGlashan. Variants of the name have been recorded since the sixteenth century. John Glessen, a Jacobite, was deported to the Chesapeake in 1747.

GLOVER. Occupational, from the once important trade of glover or glove-maker. Examples in Scotland date from the thirteenth century. James Glover, a Glasgow merchant, was trading with Virginia by 1682.

GOLDIE. A diminutive of Gold used as a surname since the sixteenth century. William Goldie, a sailor, died in Carolina around 1736.

GOLLAN. Territorial, from the lands of Gollan in Kinross-shire. Examples date from the thirteenth century. The surname was also found around Inverness. Donald Gollan, a Jacobite, was transported to the West Indies in 1747. Possibly associated with Clan Mackintosh.

GOODBRAND. Probably a corruption of an Old Norse name. A very rare name found in north-east Scotland. Alexander Goodbrand, a Jacobite from Banff, was transported to the Leeward Islands in 1747 but was liberated by the French and landed on Martinique.

GOODWILLY. An unusual surname, of unknown origin, from Fife with a few examples dating from the seventeenth century. David Goodwilly, from Cupar, was banished to America in 1752, and Joseph Goodwillie, from Kirkcaldy, settled in Vermont by 1774.

GOODWIN. A surname of Old English origin found in parts of southern Scotland from the fifteenth century. Robert Goodwin, a Covenanter from Glasgow, was transported to East New Jersey in 1685.

GORDON. Probably territorial, from the lands of Gordon in Berwickshire. Initially found in the south east but by the early fifteenth century the family was established in Aberdeenshire where it became one of the most common surnames. Several Gordons settled in America during the seventeenth century starting with George Gordon in Virginia by 1636. Clan Gordon.

GORRIE. A modified version of MacGorrie found in Perthshire since the sixteenth century. MacGorrie comes from the Gaelic name '*MacGoraidh*' which means 'son of Godfrey'. Robert Gorrie settled in East New Jersey in 1684. Clan Donald.

GORTIE. Territorial, derived from the barony of Gorthy in Perthshire. The name is uncommon but has been a surname since the thirteenth century. George Gortie, a Jacobite, was transported to Antigua in 1716.

GOUK. Possibly descriptive, a rare surname found in the vicinity of Montrose. David Gouk, a Jacobite from Montrose, was transported to Barbados in 1747.

GOURDON. Territorial, derived from Gourdon in Kincardineshire. Possibly a variant of Gordon. John Gourdon emigrated to Barbados in 1700, and Reverend John Gourdon was in Virginia by 1695.

GOURLAY. Probably territorial as it may bear the suffix *'lay'* otherwise *'law'* which is Anglo-Saxon for 'hill'. Used as a surname in east-central Scotland since the twelfth century. Reverend James Gourlay, from Stirlingshire, emigrated to the colonies in 1773

GOVAN. Territorial, derived from the lands of Govan near Glasgow. A surname found in Scotland since the thirteenth century, especially in Peebles-shire. Donald Govan, a merchant from Glasgow, was in Boston by 1684, while Thomas and William Govan were banished as Covenanters to the West Indies in 1678.

GOW. Occupational, from the Gaelic word *'gobha'* meaning 'smith'. As an occupational type name it would have been widely dispersed throughout the Highlands, however some Gows are considered part of the Clan Macpherson Donald Gow, a sheep stealer, was banished to the American colonies in 1753

GOWAN. This may be a version of *'gobha'* or possibly 'Govan'. Some Gowans claim allegiance to the Clan Donald. Donald Gowan, a Jacobite from Ross-shire, was transported to Barbados in 1747, and William Gowan was a Cromwellian transportee who settled in Maine in 1656.

GOWRIE. Territorial, taken from a district in Perthshire. Alexander Gowrie was in Boston by 1765.

GRAHAM, GRAEME. This territorial surname was introduced by Anglo-Norman knights who settled in twelfth century Scotland. It is probably derived from *'graeg ham'* Old English for 'grey house'. Found initially in the Lothians then on the Borders. Some Grahams settled in Ireland during the seventeenth century. Andrew Graham was a factor at Hudson Bay by 1770, and Patrick Graham, an apothecary from Crieff, settled in Georgia by 1736. Clan Graham.

GRAINGER. An occupational name derived from the manager of granges or farms operated for or by various abbeys. An unusual surname used since the medieval period. Margaret Grainger was transported to Maryland in 1771 and James Grainger, a physician, settled in St Kitts by 1763.

GRANT. An Anglo-Norman surname introduced into Scotland during the thirteenth century. A descriptive surname from the Old French *'le grand'* meaning 'large'.or 'great'. Most early examples in Scotland come from Strathspey in the Highlands. A considerable number of Grants were exiled to the American colonies in 1651, 1716 and 1747 due to their allegiance to the House of Stuart. Robert Grant, a farmer from Strathspey, and his family, emigrated to New York in 1774, while James Grant of Ballinvalloch was the Governor of East Florida in 1771. Clan Grant.

GRAY. Territorial, derived from a town in France. One of the Norman-French families that settled in Scotland during the thirteenth century. A common surname throughout Scotland and Ulster. John Gray, a merchant from Glasgow, settled in Port Royal, Virginia, in 1748, and James Gray, a blacksmith from Argyll, emigrated to Philadelphia in 1774. Some Gray families are affiliated to the Clan Sutherland

GREEN. Descriptive, indicating a place of residence near the 'green'. Examples date from the thirteenth century. Peter Green sailed from Islay bound for New York in 1739

GREENHILL. Descriptive indicating a place of residence. Recorded as a surname since the fifteenth century. William Greenhill, a Jacobite from Perthshire, was transported to the American colonies in 1747.

GREENLAW. Descriptive indicating a place of residence – near the 'green law' or 'green hill'. Possibly Greenlaw in Berwickshire in particular. Examples date from the twelfth century. William Greenlaw settled in Maine by 1753.

GREENLEES. Territorial, derived from the lands of Greenlees in Lanarkshire. Uncommon with examples dating from the late sixteenth century. John Greenlees, a farmer from Argyll, emigrated to North Carolina in 1774, and Peter Greenlees, was transported to Virginia in 1754.

GREG, GREGG, GREIG. A diminutive of Gregory found in east central Scotland. Reverend Thomas Greg died in the West Indies in 1699, another minister John Greig settled in Pennsylvania around

1766, and John Greg emigrated from Larne to Charleston in 1773. Clan MacGregor.

GREWER. An abbreviation of MacGruar. George Grewer, a Jacobite from Glenisla, was transported to the American colonies in 1747.

GRIER. Believed to be derived from the name MacGregor. Examples date from the sixteenth century often from Dumfries-shire. Five Covenanters from that area were banished to the American Plantations in the seventeenth century. Clan Gregor.

GRIERSON Patronymic, meaning *'son of Grier'*. Examples date from the fifteenth century and mainly come from Dumfries and Galloway. William Grierson, from Galloway, emigrated to Philadelphia in 1775. Clan Gregor

GRIEVE. Occupational signifying 'farm manager or foreman'. A surname Old English origin with most early examples coming from south east Scotland and dating from the thirteenth century. George Grieve was indentured in Chester County, Pennsylvania, in 1697, and Joseph Grieve, a weaver from Kirkcudbrightshire, and his family emigrated to Prince Edward Island in 1775.

GRIGORSON. Patronymic, meaning 'son of Gregor'. Dugald Grigorson, a farmer from Perthshire, emigrated to New York in 1775. Clan Gregor.

GRINDLAY. Derived from a place name, probably English as it bears the suffix *'lay'* alias *'law'* meaning 'hill', possibly 'green-hill'. William Grindlay was transported to the American Plantations in 1678.

GRUBB. Probably a patronymical surname derived from the Old English personal name *'Grubba'*. Found in Scotland since the early fourteenth century. Thomas Grubb, possibly from Angus, landed in East New Jersey in 1684.

GUILD. Possibly derived from the Old English personal name *'gulde'*. Early examples come from the Stirling to Edinburgh area and date from the fifteenth century. Thomas Guild, a Jacobite, was transported to South Carolina in 1716, and John Guild settled in Massachusetts in 1636.

GUIN. Possibly from *'Guinne'* the Gaelic for 'Gunn'. Christian and John Guin, from the Isle of Lewis, emigrated to Philadelphia in 1774.

GUNN. A surname of Norse origin found in Caithness since the twelfth century. Daniel or Donald Gunn was transported to Boston in 1652 and John Gunn was transported from Aberdeen to Virginia in 1754.

GUTHRIE. Territorial, derived from the barony of Guthrie in Angus. Originally *'gaothair'* a Gaelic place-name meaning 'windy place'. A surname used in Scotland since the thirteenth century. Richard Guthrie settled at Port Royal, Nova Scotia, in 1629, while John Guthrie emigrated from Montrose to East New Jersey in 1684.

HACKSTON, HAXTON. Territorial, derived from Halkerston in Midlothian. From the Old Norse *'hauk-r'* for 'hawker' and *'tun'* for 'settlement'. A rare surname found in east central Scotland. William Hackston, a Covenanter, was transported to the West Indies in 1678.

HADDOWAY. Probably a variation of the English surname 'Hathoway'. A surname recorded in Scotland since the fifteenth century in various forms. Archibald Haddoway, a Glasgow Covenanter, was transported to the West Indies in 1678.

HAGGART. A diminutive of McTaggart found in Perthshire since the sixteenth century. James 'Haddgard' was shipped to Pennsylvania in 1697 and a group of Haggarts, from Glen Coe, settled in New York in 1774.

HAIG. Possibly territorial in origin. A surname recorded in the Borders since the mid-twelfth century. Haigs were prominent among the Scots Quaker families that settled in East New Jersey in the 1680s.

HALCRO, HALCROW. Territorial, derived from the lands of Halcro in Orkney or in Caithness. Examples, localised in the Orkney Islands, exist from the late fifteenth century. Magnus Halcro, and his family, emigrated from Orkney to Georgia in 1774.

HALDANE, HADDEN. Territorial, derived from the barony of Hauden in Roxburghshire. An old surname dating from the twelfth century. George Haldane was Governor of Jamaica before 1759, and James Haldane was transported to New England in 1722.

HALIBURTON, HALYBURTON. Territorial, derived from the lands of Haliburton in Berwickshire. The name is Old English meaning *'village by the holy enclosure'.* Used as a surname since the thirteenth century. Reverend William Halyburton went to Virginia in 1766 and Robert Halyburton was in South Carolina before 1690.

HALL. A descriptive surname, based on the Old English word *'heall'*, possibly indicating a place of residence or work. It has been used as a surname since the fourteenth century. The Halls were one of the riding clans on the Borders that moved to Ulster in the seventeenth century. John Hall and his family from Renfrewshire emigrated to New England in 1775.

HALLIDAY, HOLLIDAY. A surname of unclear origin found in the Borders since the thirteenth century. Thomas Holliday settled in East New Jersey in 1684, William Holiday, a planter in Goose Creek, South Carolina, died 1781, and William Hallyday emigrated from Belfast to Philadelphia in 1771.

HAMIGAR. Territorial, taken from Hammigarth in the parish of Evie. A very rare surname from Orkney, probably of Norse origin. James Hamigar, from Evie, settled in Richmond County, Georgia, in 1775.

HAMILTON. Territorial, probably derived from a place in England, possibly in Northumberland. The surname was introduced into Scotland during the thirteenth century by an Anglo-Norman knight. Hamiltons were among the leaders of the Scots settlers during the Plantation of Ulster. Several Hamiltons emigrated to America during the colonial period – Dr Alexander Hamilton settled in Annapolis, Maryland, in 1739, William Hamilton, a highwayman, was transported to the colonies in 1749, and John Hamilton from Ireland to Philadelphia by 1752. Clan Hamilton.

HAMMEL. A territorial surname of Norman-French origin. Introduced into Scotland around 1200, and from Scotland to Ulster in the seventeenth century. Hammels from Islay settled in New York around 1739, and Alexander Hamil emigrated from Belfast to Philadelphia in 1773.

HAMPTON. Territorial, based on one of a number of place-names in England. Recorded in Scotland since the thirteenth century. John Hampton, a gardener, was among the Scots Quakers who settled in East New Jersey in the 1680s

HANCOCK. An English surname bearing the suffix *'cock'* meaning 'little', thus meaning 'little Han' or 'little John'. Very rare in Scottish records. John Hancock, a Quaker, emigrated to East New Jersey in 1685.

HANDYSIDE. Territorial, derived from a place near Berwick. Used as a surname since the fourteenth century, particularly in the eastern Borders. James Handiesyde died on the Darien Expedition of 1698, while Robert Handyside was a Jacobite transported to Montserrat in 1716.

HANNA, HANNAH, HANNAY. An old Galloway surname probably of Gaelic origin, later found throughout south-west Scotland and in Ulster. A surname used in Scotland since the late thirteenth century. William Hanna, a Covenanter, was transported to East New Jersey in 1685, Reverend William Hanna settled in Virginia in 1772, and Robert Hanna emigrated from Larne to Charleston in 1773. Clan Hannay.

HAPPY. A surname of unknown origin, perhaps a descriptive one. Francis Happy was in Boston by 1698.

HARDCASS. A variant of HARCARSE, a surname based on the lands of that name in Berwickshire. Used as a surname since the early thirteenth century. John Hardcass was in Boston by 1718.

HARDIE, HARDY. A descriptive surname, based on the Old French *'le hardi'* signifying 'the brave'. Probably an Anglo-Norman surname introduced in the reign of King David. The name is found throughout Scotland and its use there can be dated from the thirteenth century. A few Hardies from Aberdeen were among the Scots pioneers in East New Jersey during the 1680s. Some claim allegiance to either Clan Ferguson or Clan Mackintosh.

HARKNESS. Possibly of Scandinavian origin as the suffix *'ness'* means 'headland'. The surname which can be traced back to the sixteenth tended to be localised in Dumfries-shire and later in Ireland. John Harkness, a Covenanter, was banished to the American Plantations in 1684.

HARLEY. Probably territorial from one of a number of places named Harlaw. An Old English name bearing the suffix *'law'* meaning 'hill'. Used as a surname since the thirteenth century. Adam and James Harley were Glasgow weavers who sailed for New York in 1774.

HARPER. An occupational surname found in Scotland since the late thirteenth century. In the *Gaeltacht* it appears as 'Chlarsair' or 'MacChruiter'. Some Harpers are linked with Clan Buchanan. Thomas Harper was indentured in Chester County, Pennsylvania, in 1697, and John Harper, a Covenanter from Ayrshire, was transported to New York in 1684. Clan Buchanan.

HARRIS. A patronymic meaning 'Harry's son'. Not too common in
Scotland. John Harris emigrated to East New Jersey in 1685, while
Robert Harris, from Edinburgh, was married in New York in 1695.
HARRISON. An English patronymic surname, meaning 'son of Harry',
found in Scotland since the early modern era. David Harrison, a
wheelwright from Ecclefechan, and his family settled on Prince
Edward Island in 1775.
HARROWER. A rare surname of occupational origin, based on the
agricultural task of harrowing. Traditionally found along the east
coast of Scotland since the thirteenth century. John Harrower, a
tutor from the Shetland Islands, settled in Fredericksburg, Virginia,
in 1774.
HART. A surname of English origin found in Scotland since the late
thirteenth century. John Hart, a mason from Glasgow, emigrated to
New York in 1775.
HARVEY, HARVIE. A name from Brittany introduced into England by
the Normans and found in Scotland as a surname since the
fourteenth century and in Ulster by the seventeenth century. Thomas
Harvie, from Glasgow, was transported to Maryland in 1704 and
Daniel Harvey, a gardener, sailed for Philadelphia in 1774.
HASTIE, HAISTIE, HEASTIE. A surname of unknown origin found in
Scotland since the fourteenth century. John Heastie emigrated to
Charleston in 1774, and Ann Hastie was banished to the American
colonies in 1760.
HASTINGS. Territorial, from the town of Hastings in England. A branch
of the family moved to Scotland during the reign of William the
Lion and settled in Angus. John Hastings, a skipper from
Prestonpans, died in Virginia in 1707. Clan Campbell.
HATMAKER. A rare surname of occupational origin. Early examples
are found in eastern Scotland from Leith to Inverness. Magdalene
Hatmaker settled in East New Jersey in 1685.
HAY. A Norman name, probably of territorial origin, introduced into
Scotland in the twelfth century. Most early examples come from
Perthshire. James and Thomas Hay were members of the Scots
Charitable Society of Boston in the 1690s, and Archibald Hay was a
planter in Barbados before 1652.
HAZEL. Possibly territorial from Haswell in County Durham. Found as
'Haswell' in Scotland since the thirteenth century, and later as

Hazel. W. Hazel, a Scots indentured servant, absconded in South Carolina during 1737.

HECKLE. Possibly a Dutch surname. Robert Heckle, a mason, emigrated to New York in 1774.

HECTOR. A patronymical surname which was taken from classical sources. An unusual surname in Scotland where examples date from the sixteenth century. John Hector, a Jacobite from Aberdeen, was transported to the Chesapeake in 1747.

HEDDERWICK, HEDDERICK. Territorial, from one or more places on the east coast of Scotland, derived from the Old Norse 'hader wic' meaning 'settlement among the heather'. A surname used in Scotland since the sixteenth century. James and William Hedderick were prisoners of war transported to Boston by Cromwell in 1652.

HEDDLE. Territorial, derived from the lands of Heddle in Orkney. A local surname in the Orkney Islands since the fifteenth century. Alexander Heddle, from Shapinsay, emigrated to Georgia in 1774.

HENDERSON. Patronymic, meaning 'son of Hendry (Henry)', a common surname in Scotland. Examples date from the fourteenth century. Originally found on the Borders and later in Fife and Caithness. A Thomas Henderson, from Fife, is claimed to have been among the first settlers of Virginia. James Henderson arrived in York County, Virginia, in 1666, and James Henderson emigrated from Ireland to Pennsylvania by 1769. Some Hendersons are allied to Clan Gunn and others to Clan Donald.

HENDRY, HENRY. Patronymic from the forename 'Henry'. A surname recorded in Scotland since the sixteenth century. Neil Hendry, a tailor from Kintyre, settled in North Carolina in 1774, and Reverend Patrick Henry, from Aberdeenshire, settled in Hanover County, Virginia, in 1732. Some Henrys link with Clan McNaughton others to Clan Donald.

HENSHAW. Territorial, probably taken from an English place-name. William Henshaw, a Glasgow merchant and Covenanter, was transported to the West Indies in 1678.

HEPBURN. Territorial, derived from the lands of Hebburn in Northumberland. It was brought from England during the middle of the twelfth century and could be found in East Lothian since then. Charles Hepburn, a merchant from Glasgow, settled at Cape Fear, North Carolina, by 1741, Mary Hepburn, from Edinburgh, was transported to Maryland in 1704, and Samuel Hepburn emigrated from Londonderry to Philadelphia in 1786.

HERCULES. Possibly a variant of 'Herkless' a surname of territorial origin derived from 'Erchless' in Kiltarlity, Inverness-shire, or of 'Hercas' derived from 'Harcarse' in Berwickshire. James Hercules was indentured in Chester County, Pennsylvania, in 1697, and William Hercules, a weaver from Paisley, emigrated to New York in 1774.

HERD. A surname of occupational origin used in Scotland since the medieval period. John Herd, a Jacobite, was transported to South Carolina in 1716.

HERDMAN, HERMAN. Possibly of Flemish origin. A rare name with a few examples in eastern Scotland since the fifteenth century. Reverend James Herdman settled in Henrico County, Virginia, in 1770.

HERIOT, HERRIOT. Territorial, derived from the lands of Heriot in Midlothian. Examples date from the twelfth century and tend to be localised around Edinburgh. Captain Richard Heriot was one of the leaders of the Scots in Nova Scotia during the 1620s.

HERON, HERRING. A Borders surname, possibly descriptive, found there since the thirteenth century. During the seventeenth century a number of Border reivers, including Herons, moved to Ulster. James Herron and his family, emigrated from Kirkcudbrightshire to New York in 1774, and Janet Herring, a Jacobite, was exiled to Maryland in 1747.

HEUGH. Descriptive, used to indicate a place of residence. A heugh or haugh is a mound or raised land by a river. Andrew Heugh, from Stirlingshire, was a planter in Montgomery County, Maryland, before 1771.

HEWATT, HOWAT. A diminutive of Hugh based on the French name 'huet'. A name found in Scotland since the fifteenth century. Reverend Alexander Hewatt settled in Charleston in 1763, and Dr James Hewett was in Boston by 1713.

HIGGINS. Probably from the Irish Gaelic surname 'O'hUiginn'. A surname found in Scotland since the seventeenth century. George Higgins, a Covenanter from Linlithgow, was banished to Carolina in 1684

HILL. English, descriptive, originally used to identify a resident on a hill. Examples date from the thirteenth century can be found throughout the Lowlands. Some of the Hills in Ulster may be descended from Scottish immigrants. Janet Hill, from Edinburgh, was transported to Virginia in 1696, and Thomas Hill was a member of the Scots Charitable Society of Boston in 1686.

HISLOP, HYSLOP. A descriptive name bearing the English suffix *'hope'* meaning 'valley', from 'Hesilhope' thus possibly meaning 'hazel-valley'. Examples in Scotland date from the fifteenth century. James Hislop was a member of the Scots Charitable Society of Boston in 1699, and Robert Hyslop was a merchant in New York by 1773.

HODGE, HODGEON. Patronymic, diminutives of Rodger. Found in Scotland since the sixteenth century. Adam Hodgeon, a Covenanter, was transported to Carolina in 1684, and Robert Hodge settled in Philadelphia in 1770.

HOGG. The origins of this surname are unclear. Possibly it is a descriptive name referring to an animal, or it could be from a place as some early examples use *'del Hoga'*, or even from the Gaelic word *'ogg'* meaning 'young'. In Scotland the earliest examples are found in the south east and date from the thirteenth century. Several Hoggs were transported to New England in 1651 on the orders of Oliver Cromwell.

HOLLAND. Territorial, taken from one of a number of places in Orkney and Shetland or in England. Possibly derived from the Danish *'hoi land'* meaning 'high-land'. An uncommon name recorded in Scotland since the fifteenth century. Thomas Holland, a Jacobite, was transported to the colonies in 1716, and William Holland took part in the Darien Expedition of 1699.

HOME, HUME. Territorial, derived from the barony of Home in Berwickshire. A surname, especially in the south-east, since the twelfth century. Sir George Home settled at Port Royal, Nova Scotia, by 1630, and a number of Homes were transported to the American colonies as prisoners of war in 1651, 1716 and 1747.

HONEYMAN. A Flemish surname found in Fife since the sixteenth century. Three clergymen and one physician of that name and all from Kincardineshire settled in America during the eighteenth century.

HOOD. An abbreviated verion of the Anglo-Saxon personal name *'Huda'* recorded in Scotland since the early thirteenth century. Adam Hood, a Covenanter, was transported to East New Jersey in 1685, Peter Hood was indentured in Pennsylvania in 1697, and John Hood emigrated from Belfast to Philadelphia in 1773.

HOOK. A descriptive surname indicating a place of residence on 'a spit of land'. Old English in origin but found in south west Scotland since the thirteenth century. Jane and Robert Hooks settled in East New Jersey in 1684.

HOOPER. Occupational, derived from the job of making hoops or bands to encircle barrel staves. Found in south east Scotland from the thirteenth century. Reverend William Hooper from Berwickshire emigrated to New England in 1747.

HOPE. Derived from an Old English word meaning 'enclosed land'. Used as a surname in south east Scotland since the thirteenth century. Archibald Hope settled in Pennsylvania during 1677, and John Hope, a merchant from Glasgow, was in Osborne and Halifax, Virginia, before the American Revolution.

HORN. An Old English name recorded in Scotland since the thirteenth century. Alexander Horn died in South Carolina in 1777 and Sophia Horne settled in New Jersey before 1747.

HORNER. Occupational, based on the job of horn spoon maker. Relatively uncommon in Scotland but examples date from the fifteenth century. Barbara Horner, a Covenanter, was banished to the American Plantations in 1684.

HORSBURGH. Territorial, derived from the lands of Horsburgh in Peebles-shire. A surname recorded in Scotland since the thirteenth century. Alexander Horsburgh, a merchant from Glasgow, was in Virginia before the Revolution, and Dr William Horsburgh died in New Providence before 1763.

HOSIE. Probably territorial, possibly derived from Houssaye in Normandy. William Hosie, a woolcomber in Aberdeen, was transported to Virginia for conspiracy in 1772.

HOSSACK. A Gaelic name found in the vicinity of Inverness since around 1500. Janet Hossack was indentured in Chester County, Pennsylvania, in 1698, and Thomas Husk was a drummer of the Pennsylvania Regiment in 1749.

HOUSTOUN, HOUSTON. Territorial, derived from the lands of Houstoun, meaning 'Hugh's toun or settlement', in Renfrewshire. Established as a surname in the thirteenth century. In Ulster some Uisdeans or Huisdeans or MacUisdins, septs of Clan Donald, may have adopted the name 'Houstoun'. Patrick Houstoun, a merchant from Glasgow, was one of the leaders of the Scots settlers in Georgia in the 1730s, and William Houstoun from Donegal participated in the Darien Expedition of 1699.

HOW. A surname of unknown origin recorded in Scotland since the twelfth century. Daniel How was transported to Boston in 1651 and James How was in Boston by 1693.

HOWATSON. Patronymic, signifying 'son of little Hugh'. A surname in Scotland since the sixteenth century. James Howatson, a Covenanter from Dumfries-shire, was banished to the American Plantations in 1684.

HOWIE, HUIE. Descriptive, from the Gaelic surname *'MacIlghuie'*, originally 'Mac Gille dhuibh' meaning 'son of the black lad'. Reverend Alexander Howie from Aberdeen settled in Pennsylvania in 1730, and John Howie was transported to Barbados in 1665. Clan Donald.

HOWNAM. Territorial, from the lands of Hounam in Roxburghshire. An unusual surname with a few examples dating from the seventeenth century. Walter Howname, a Covenanter from Teviotdale, was transported to Port Royal, Jamaica, in 1685.

HUGHES. Patronymic, meaning 'son of Hugh'. Mary Hughes, an indentured servant from Glasgow, emigrated via London to Maryland in 1775.

HUNTER. A surname of occupational origin found in Scotland since the twelfth century. George Hunter was the Surveyor General until his death in Charleston in 1755, and Dr William Hunter (1730-1777) died in Rhode Island.

HURRY. Territorial, derived from the lands of Harray in Orkney. John Hurry, a farmer from Orkney, settled in Richmond County, Georgia, in 1774.

HUTCHEON, HUTCHISON, HUTCHESON. Patronymic, based on the forename 'Hugh' or the French *'Huchon'*. Used widely in Scotland since the fifteenth century. Reverend Alexander Hutcheson emigrated in 1722 and settled in Bohemia Manor, Maryland. Some are connected with Clan Donald.

HUTTON. Territorial, derived from one of a number of places of that name. Examples date from the thirteenth century. Alexander Hutton settled in East New Jersey by 1690, and Thomas Hutton, from Berwickshire, emigrated to Maryland in 1684.

HYNDMAN. Occupational, signifying 'a man responsible for hinds'. Early examples come from west central Scotland. Andrew Hyndman and his family from Argyll emigrated to North Carolina in 1774.

IMLAY. An abbreviated version of the Gaelic name *'Imlach'*. Most early examples come from north-east Scotland and date from the early fifteenth century. Jean Imlay was transported from Aberdeen to Virginia in 1753.

IMRIE, IMBRIE. Derived from a surname introduced from Flanders in the fourteenth century. Duncan Imrie, a ship's carpenter from Dundee, settled in Carolina before the American Revolution, and John Imbrie, a merchant from Falkland, was in New York by 1778.

INCH, INCHES. Derived from the Gaelic word *'innis'* meaning 'island'. A surname since the thirteenth century. Thomas Inch was in Boston by 1716. Clan Donnachaidh.

INGLIS. The Old Scots word for *'English'* found used as a surname in Scotland since the thirteenth century. William Inglis was transported to Carolina in 1684, and Mungo Inglis was a tutor at the College of William and Mary from 1694 to 1705.

INGRAM. Derived from an Old English personal name and used as a surname in Scotland since the fourteenth century. James Ingram, settled as a merchant in Virginia by 1769.

INNES. Territorial, derived from the barony of Innes in Moray and based on *'innis'* the Gaelic word for 'island'. The family was founded by an immigrant from Flanders named Berowald in the twelfth century. A common surname in northern Scotland. Reverend Robert Innes emigrated to Virginia in 1677 and Dr Walter Innes was admitted to the Scots Charitable Society of Boston in 1699. Clan Innes.

IRELAND. This surname has diverse origins. It may indicate (1) a person from the island of Ireland, (2) it may be a local place name, indicating 'lands lying to the west', or (3) it may come from the Old

Norse words *'eyrr-land'* meaning 'gravelly-beach'. It has been used as a surname since the thirteenth century. John Ireland, a Covenanter, was transported to Jamaica in 1685, and David Ireland settled in Pennsylvania during 1773.

IRONSIDE. Territorial, derived from a place-name in Aberdeenshire. An unusual name localised in north-east Scotland. Christian Ironside, was banished from Aberdeen to the American colonies in 1749.

IRVINE, IRWIN. Territorial, derived from Irvine in Ayrshire. Examples date from the medieval period. James Irvine, a Jacobite from Nithsdale, was transported to Port Oxford, Maryland, in 1747, another James Irvine, this time from the Orkney Islands, emigrated to Georgia in 1775, and Agnes Irwin emigrated from Belfast to Philadelphia in 1773.

IRVING. Territorial, derived from Irving in Dumfries-shire. Also dating from the medieval period. William Irving settled in Virginia before 1765

ISBISTER. Territorial, from a place in the Orkney Islands. Recorded there since the sixteenth century. Hugh Isbister settled in Richmond County, Georgia, in 1775.

IVAR. An Anglicised version of the Gaelic name *'Imhaer'* derived from the Norse forename 'Ivarr'. A localised name found in Argyll. John and Malcolm Ivar, Covenanters, were banished to the American Plantations in 1685. Clan Campbell.

JACK. Patronymic, based on the French forename *'Jacques'*. which has been used as a surname in Scotland since the fifteenth century. John and Janet Jack, from Moray, emigrated to Philadelphia in 1775, and Robert Jack was indentured in Chester County, Pennsylvania, in 1697.

JACKSON. A patronymic, 'son of Jack', is found throughout the British Isles but is relatively more common in England. The surname has been recorded in Scotland since the fifteenth century. Patrick Jackson, from Dunbar, was a merchant in Virginia by 1669, and William Jackson, a husbandman from Peebles, settled in Maryland in 1735.

JAFFRAY, JEFFREY. Patronymic, derived from a Norman-French variation of the Anglo-Saxon name *'Godfrey'*. A surname found in

Scotland since the fifteenth century. William Jeffrey, from Perth, died in Philadelphia in 1758.

JAMIE. Patronymic, a diminutive of 'James'. Relatively uncommon but a few examples date from the sixteenth century. Robert Jamie, from Montrose, was transported to the colonies in 1775.

JAMIESON. Patronymic – the 'son of James' – used as a surname since the fifteenth century. David, Neil, and Patrick Jamieson, prisoners of war, were transported to Boston in 1651.

JAPP. A Dutch or Flemish surname, based on the Biblical name Job, introduced into Scotland in the medieval period. Relatively uncommon. John Japp, a Jacobite from Banff, was transported to the West Indies in 1747.

JARDINE. Possibly descriptive, used to describe someone who lived in or by a garden. Examples of the surname tend to be localised on the Borders and date from the twelfth century. Andrew Jardine, a Covenanter, was transported to the colonies in 1685, and William Jarden, a merchant from Dumfries, was admitted to the Scots Charitable Society of Boston in 1684. Clan Jardine.

JARVIE, JERVY. An abbreviation of the name Jarvis alias Gervaise, a Norman French name which arrived via England by the thirteenth century. John Jervy, a wright from Falkirk, was transported to the West Indies in 1678.

JOHNSON. Patronymic meaning '*son of John*' – a common surname throughout the British Isles. Scottish examples date from the fourteenth century. Gavin Johnson, a schoolmaster from Edinburgh, emigrated to Prince Edward Island in 1775, and James Johnson was admitted to the Scots Charitable Society of Boston in 1665.

JOHNSTON, JOHNSTONE. Territorial, derived from the lands of Johnstone in Annandale, Dumfries-shire. 'Johnstone', '*the tun or settlement of John*' was established around 1174, and within a generation the surname 'de Jonistune' appears on documents. John Johnston, a druggist from Edinburgh, settled in East New Jersey in 1685 and was later the Mayor of New York, Reverend Gideon Johnston went to Carolina in 1707, an James Johnston was an indentured servant in Philadelphia during 1769. Clan Johnstone.

JOINER, JUNOR, JENNER. An very uncommon occupational surname in Scotland, possibly from the Middle English word '*engynour*' meaning 'engineer'. Most of the few early examples come from

Inverness-shire. David Joiner, a Jacobite from Aberdeen, was transported to the West Indies in 1747, and William Junor, a robber from Aberdeenshire, was transported to the colonies in 1763.

JOSS. Possibly originally a Breton personal name introduced into Scotland by the Anglo-Normans. In Ireland it appears as 'Joyce'. Margaret Joss was transported to Virginia in 1752.

JUNKEIN. A Flemish surname meaning *'little John'*. James Junkein from Kilmacolm was banished to the American Plantations in 1670, and Robert Junkins, a Cromwellian prisoner, was transported to New England in 1650.

KANE, KEIN. An abbreviation of the surname Gaelic *'MacKean'* meaning 'son of John'. Patrick Kein was transported to the American colonies in 1679, and Hugh Cane, a Jacobite, was transported to Virginia in 1716. Clan Donald or Clan Gunn.

KAY, KEAY. This surname may have been introduced from northern England in the medieval period but most Kays or Keays in Scotland result from the Gaelic prefix *'Mac'* being dropped, however others claim descent from the *clan dhai'*. Alexander Kay, a piper from Breadalbane, emigrated to New York in 1775. Kay therefore may be part of Clan Mackay or Clan Dhai - a member of the Clan Chattan Confederation.

KEIR. Territorial, derived from the lands of Keir in Stirlingshire. A surname recorded since the thirteenth century. Alexander Keir settled in New Jersey by 1737, and Alexander Keith, from Banff, was transported to America in 1766.

KEITH. Territorial, derived from the lands of Keith in East Lothian. Early examples come from south –east Scotland but latterly mostly from the north east. Reverend James Keith settled in Fauquier County, Virginia, before 1645, and George Keith was prominent among the Scots Quakers of early East New Jersey. Clan Keith or Clan Sutherland.

KELLIE, KELLY. Territorial, derived from places in Angus, Fife or Renfrewshire. Derived from the Gaelic word *'coille'* meaning 'a wood'. A surname used since the fourteenth century. John and Catherine Kelly, Covenanters, were banished to the American Plantations in 1685. Some Kellies are linked to Clan Donald.

KELLO. Territorial, derived from the lands of Kelloe in Berwickshire. Used as a surname in Scotland since the thirteenth century. John Kello, a Covenanter, was banished to Carolina in 1684.

KELMAN, KILMAN. Territorial, derived from a place in Aberdeenshire. Probably a Gaelic name bearing the prefix *'Kil'* or *'cill'* meaning 'cell' or 'church'. William Kilman, a blacksmith, emigrated to Virginia in 1773.

KELSO. Territorial, derived from the burgh of Kelso in Roxburghshire. Examples date from around 1200 AD. William Kelso, a surgeon-apothecary from Ayr, a Covenanter and rebel, fled via Ulster to Boston in 1680, and Robert Kelso was in Boston by 1732.

KELTON. Territorial, derived from a place-name in Kirkcudbrightshire. A rare surname. Thomas Kelton, a Cromwellian prisoner of war, was transported to Boston in 1650.

KELVIE. An abbreviation of the Gaelic surname *'Mac Shealbhaigh'* anglicised to 'McKelvie'. William Kelvie emigrated to Maryland in 1739. Clan Campbell.

KEMLO. Origin unclear, possibly a diminutive of *'Kemloch'* and thus probably a variant of *'Kinloch'*. A very unusual surname. Joseph Kemlo, a Jacobite from Aberdeen, was transported to Maryland in 1747.

KEMP. Descriptive, from the Old Norse for *'warrior'*. Examples date from the fifteenth century. William Kemp emigrated to Philadelphia in 1775, and Daniel Kemp was exiled to Boston in 1651.

KENNAN. An abbreviation of *'McKennan'* a local surname in Galloway. Examples date from the sixteenth century. William Kennan, from Dumfries, died in Richmond, Virginia, in 1765.

KENNEDY. Descriptive, from the Gaelic word *'Ceannaideach'* meaning 'grim-headed'. A surname found in south-west Scotland since the twelfth century. John Kennedy was transported to Virginia in 1666, Archibald Kennedy, the Receiver General of Customs, died in New York in 1763, and Thomas Kennedy was an Irish indentured servant in Pennsylvania in 1785.. Clan Kennedy.

KENNIBURGH. Possibly derived from the Anglo-Saxon word *'Cynesburh'* meaning the 'royal stronghold'. John Kenniburgh emigrated to North Carolina in 1775.

KENNOUGH, KENNY. Patronymic, derived from the Gaelic name *'Coinneach'* equivalent to 'Kenneth'. Examples date from the fourteenth century. Alexander Kennough, a Jacobite, was transported to the colonies in 1747, and John Kennie left for East New Jersey in 1685.

KENT. Territorial, derived from Kent in England. A surname in Scotland since the twelfth century. Andrew Kent, a dyer from Galloway, emigrated to the American colonies in 1722.

KER, KERR. One of the oldest Borders surnames, dating from the twelfth century. Possibly derived from the Old Norse *'kjarr'* meaning 'marsh dweller'. During the seventeenth century Border reiver families including Kerrs took refuge in Ulster. John Kerr was a surgeon on Charleton Island, Hudson Bay, in 1681, while Donald Kerr, a Covenanter, was deported to New England in 1685. Clan Kerr.

KIDD. Patronymic, a diminutive of 'Christopher' or a variant of 'Kitt'. A surname found in Angus and Perth since the fourteenth century. Captain William Kidd, a shipmaster from Dundee, settled in New York in 1688.

KILGOUR. Territorial, derived from a place in central Fife. Used as a surname since the sixteenth century. The prefix *'Kil'* comes from the Gaelic word *'ceall'* meaning 'cell'or 'church'. John Kilgour, a Covenanter from Livingstone, was transported to Carolina in 1684, and a John Kilgore settled in Maine by 1764.

KILLOCH. Territorial, originating with a place name in Ayrshire and used as a surname since the seventeenth century. Probably derived from a Gaelic term *'coil loch'* meaning 'wood by the lake' William Killoch, from Renfrewshire, was in Boston by 1762

KILPATRICK. Territorial, based on a place in Dunbartonshire. Derived from a Gaelic term meaning *'the church of (St) Patrick'*. A surname used in Scotland since the thirteenth century, also found in Ulster. Robert Kilpatrick was a minister in Newfoundland and in New York from 1730 to 1741, and John Kilpatrick emigrated from Belfast to Philadelphia in 1773.

KIMMINGS. Possibly a variant of Cummings – a surname derived from Comines in Flanders. Alexander Kimmings, from Stranraer, died in New Jersey by 1784. Clan Cummings.

KINAMONT, KINNINMONTH. Territorial, from the lands of Kininmonth in Fife. Based on a Gaelic name *'cinn fhionn monaidh'* meaning 'at the head of the white hill'. A surname in use since the thirteenth century. Ambrose Kinamont was in Annapolis, Maryland, by 1699.

KINCAID. Territorial, derived from the lands of Kincaid in Stirlingshire. Based on a Gaelic place name *'ceann cadha'* meaning 'head of the pass'. A surname used in Scotland since the fifteenth century. John Kincaid, a Covenanter, was transported to East New Jersey in 1685, and David Kincaid was admitted to the Scots Charitable Society of Boston in 1684.

KING. A surname found in Scotland but of unknown origin. Examples date back to the thirteenth century. James King, a Jacobite, was transported to Maryland in 1747, and Patrick King, from Edinburgh, was bound for New York in 1775.

KINLOCH. Territorial, derived from the lands of Kinloch in Fife. Based on a Gaelic place name *'ceann loch'* meaning 'at the head of the lake'. Examples of the surname date from 1200 AD. Alexander and James Kinloch, settled as merchants in Charleston during the late 1720s.

KINNAIRD. Territorial, derived from the barony of Kinnaird in Perthshire. Based on a Gaelic place name *'ceann aird'* meaning 'at the head of a height' or 'summit'. A surname in Scotland since the thirteenth century. Sir Alexander Kinnaird died at Darien in 1699.

KINNEAR. Territorial, derived from the lands of Kinnear in north east Fife. Based on the Gaelic place name *'ceann iar'* meaning 'head(land) in the west'. Examples date from the thirteenth century. Jane Kanere arrived in York County, Virginia, in 1666, and John Kinnear arrived, with his family, in New York during 1774.

KINNELL. Territorial, derived from Kinnell in Angus. Based on the Gaelic place name *'ceann alla'* meaning 'head of the crag'. An uncommon surname. The earliest recording from the fourteenth century. William Kinnell, a tailor, emigrated to Darien in 1698.

KIRBY, KIRKBY. Territorial, derived from one of a number of places of that name in Scotland or northern England. Possibly from the Danish *'kirk by'* meaning 'church-settlement'. Thomas Alexander Kirby settled in Massachusetts around 1720.

KIRK. Descriptive, indicating residence by a church or kirk. A common surname in Scotland since the fifteenth century. Margaret Kirk was transported to Virginia in 1696.

KIRKCALDY. Territorial, derived from the town in Fife. Origin unclear, possibly from '*caer – culdee*' the 'fort of the Culdees'. Used as a surname since the thirteenth century. Margaret Carkawdy was in Northumberland County, Virginia, by 1651.

KIRKLAND. Descriptive, indicating residence on kirk or church land. Derived from one of a number of places so named in Scotland or northern England. John Kirkland left Leith bound for East New Jersey in 1685.

KIRKPATRICK. Territorial, signifying '*the church of (Saint) Patrick*', derived from one of a number of places in Galloway. A surname recorded since around 1200. Reverend Henry Kirkpatrick was sent to the Leeward Islands in 1768, and Samuel Kirkpatrick, from Londonderry, was admitted to the Scots Charitable Society of Boston in 1694. Clan Colquhoun.

KIRKWALL. Territorial, probably derived from Kirkwall in the Orkney Islands. Based on the Old Norse *kirkin-vagr*' meaning 'church on the bay'. Elizabeth Kirkwall was transported to Jamaica in 1685.

KIRKWOOD. Descriptive, derived from one of a number of places in southern Scotland. Examples date from the sixteenth century. John and William Kirkwood emigrated to Boston in 1736.

KISAACH. Patronymic, possibly derived from the Gaelic name '*Cessoc*' , or an abbreviation of '*MacKessock*' meaning 'son of Isaac'. John Kisaach, a Jacobite from Moray, was transported to the West Indies in 1747. Clan Campbell.

KNEELAND. Territorial, derived from the lands of Kneeland (now Cleland) in Lanarkshire. Three Kneelands were among the members of the Scots Charitable Society of Boston in the seventeenth century.

KNOX. Territorial, from the lands of Knock in Renfrewshire, and based on the Gaelic word '*cnoc*' meaning 'hill'. A surname recorded in Scotland since the thirteenth century and in Ireland at a later date. Thomas Knox, from Aberdeenshire, was transported to Virginia in 1775, and Reverend Hugh Knox settled in St Croix by 1773.

KYLE. Territorial, from the lands of Kyle in Ayrshire, probably based on the Gaelic word '*caol*' meaning 'strait'. Early examples tend to come from Ayrshire. The name is also found in Ulster. Forbes Kyle, a coach wheeler, emigrated to Maryland in 1774.

LAIDLAW, LAIDLIE. Territorial, possibly from a place near Galashiels. A Borders surname dating from the thirteenth century. Walter

Ladley emigrated to Jamaica in 1730, and Archibald Laidlie was a
minister in New York from 1734 to 1776.

LAING, LANG. Descriptive, from the Old English word *'lang'* meaning
'long'. A standard Lowland Scots surname dating back to the
thirteenth century. William Laing, a Covenanter from Hawick, was
transported to New York in 1684, while Alexander Lang, a weaver
from Paisley, emigrated to Nevis in 1774. Some Langs belong to
Clan Gayre, other to Clan Leslie or Clan Donnachaidh.

LAIRD. Probably occupational meaning 'land-owner'. A surname in
Scotland since the thirteenth century. Katherine Laird was
transported to York County, Virginia, in 1666, and Samuel Laird, a
minister in Londonderry, emigrated to North Carolina in 1755.

LAMB. A Flemish name found in Scotland since the thirteenth century.
James Lamb, a Jacobite, was transported to the West Indies in 1747,
and William Lamb emigrated to Jamaica in 1774.

LAMBIE. A diminutive of 'Lamb' found mainly in Angus since the
thirteenth century. William Lambie died in Jamaica before 1769.

LAMOND, LAMONT. Occupational, derived from an Old Norse term
for 'lawmaker'. A surname associated with Argyll since the
thirteenth century. John and Joseph Lamond were Jacobites
transported to Maryland in 1747. Clan Lamont.

LANG. A descriptive surname based on the Anglo-Saxon word for
'long'. A surname in Scotland since the thirteenth century. George
Lang, from Glasgow, settled in Virginia by 1763, and William Lang
was a runaway seaman in Virginia during 1752.

LAPLEY. Possibly a variant of Lapsley, a surname recorded in
Stirlingshire since the seventeenth century. George and Patrick
Lapley, joiners, emigrated to Boston in 1764.

LATTO, LATTA, LAUTTIE. Territorial, derived from the lands of
Laithis in Ayrshire, and used as a surname since the fourteenth
century. William Latta, a joinere, settled in New England in 1764.

LAUDER. Territorial, derived from the burgh of Lauder in Berwickshire.
Examples of the surname date from the thirteenth century and
mainly come from south-east Scotland. Reverend Francis Lauder
settled in Maryland in 1761, while William Lauder, from
Stirlingshire, was transported there in 1729.

LAURIE, LAWRIE, LOWRY. Patronymic, a diminutive of Laurence. Gavin Lawrie was the Deputy Governor of East New Jersey from 1684, and William Lowry died in Elizabeth City, Virginia, in 1687.

LAW. Descriptive, from the Old English word *'law'* meaning 'hill', thus indicating a person's place of residence. Used as a surname in Scotland since the fifteenth century. John Law [1671-1729] from Edinburgh, was the promoter of the French Mississippi Company.

LAWSON. Patronymic, signifying *'son of Law or Lawrence'*, a surname used since the fourteenth century. Reverend Robert Lawson, from Dumfries-shire, died in Pennsylvania in 1712, and Marion Lawson was transported to New York in 1682.

LAWTON, LAUGHTON. Descriptive, indicating place of residence, from *'law tun'* meaning 'settlement on a hill'.
Patrick Laughton, from Kirkwall, was a gunner's mate on the St Andrew bound for Darien in 1698, and Alexander Lawton, a Jacobite, was transported to St Kitts in 1716.

LEACY. Probably a version of the Norman surname *'Lacy'*. George Leacy was in Pennsylvania by 1693.

LEAL. A rare surname of unknown origin with examples dating from the fifteenth century, mainly in north east Scotland. Anne Leal from Caithness, settled in Richmond County, Georgia, in 1775.

LEARMONTH. Territorial, derived from Learmonth in Berwickshire. Most early examples come from south east Scotland dating from the fifteenth century. Alexander Lermonth emigrated to East New Jersey in 1685, and Euphame Learmonth settled in Philadelphia in 1775.

LECKIE, LACKIE, LUCKIE. Territorial, derived from the barony of Leckie in Stirlingshire. Leckie probably is based on a Gaelic word *leacach'* meaning 'hillside'. A surname since the fifteenth century. Andrew Leckie, a labourer from Glasgow, emigrated to New York in 1775, John Lucky, a Jacobite, was deported to Maryland in 1747. Clan MacGregor.

LEES. Possibly derived from McLeish. John Lees was transported from Glasgow to Virginia in 1773

LEGG. An unusual surname, possibly Old English, found in north-east Scotland since the sixteenth century. John Leg, from Banff, died in Jamaica in 1764.

LEGGETT, LEGET. Patronymic or possibly occupational. If the former it may be a diminutive of the Old English forename *Leodgeard'*, alternatively it comes from the post of legate or envoy. It appears as a surname in Scotland since the fifteenth century. William Leget was in New York by 1763.

LEIGHTON. Territorial, derived from the barony of Leighton in Bedfordshire, England, probably introduced into Scotland by the Anglo-Normans during the twelfth century. S. Leighton, a clerk from Edinburgh, settled in Georgia in 1775.

LEIPER. Occupational, based on the Old English word *'leapere'* meaning 'basket-maker'. A very old surname in Scotland which has been used since the twelfth century. Dr James Leiper was buried in Philadelphia in 1771, and Thomas Leiper emigrated to Maryland in 1763.

LEISHMAN. Possibly an Old English occupational name indicating a farmworker, from *''lees'* meaning 'field', and 'man'. James Leishman was in Boston by 1717, and John Leishman, from Falkirk, died in Maine during 1780.

LEITCH, LEACH. Occupational, derived from the Old English word *laece'* meaning 'doctor'. A surname in Scotland since the fourteenth century. David Leitch, a vagabond, was ordered to be transported to the American Plantations in 1671, and Robert Leitch, a farmer, emigrated to New York in 1774.

LEITH. Territorial, derived from the burgh of Leith. Used as a surname since the fourteenth century. Alexander Leith, a merchant, died in Philadelphia before 1750, and Thomas Leith arrived in South Carolina in 1682.

LENDRUM. Territorial, derived from Lendrum in Aberdeenshire, probably a Gaelic word bearing the prefix *'leann'* meaning 'marsh' followed by *'drum'* signifying 'ridge'. A very rare surname. Thomas Lendrum settled in Port Royal, Virginia, before 1784.

LENNOX. Territorial, derived from the district of Lennox. The place name is based on the Gaelic word *'leamhanach'* which means 'the place abounding with elms'. A surname found in Scotland since the fifteenth century. James Lenox, the son of a Scots immigrant, was the co-founder of the New York Public Library. Another James Lennox was a merchant in Charleston before 1765.

LENY, LENNIE. A name based on the lands of Leny near Callander and used as a surname since the thirteenth century. Possibly from the Gaelic word *'leana'* meaning 'a marsh'. William Lenney, from Orkney, was in Boston by 1750. Clan Buchanan.

LESLIE, LESLEY. Territorial, derived from the barony of Leslie in Fife, and used as a surname since the thirteenth century. Andrew Leslie was the minister of St Paul's, South Carolina, from 1729 to 1740, and Margaret Leslie was a Covenanter banished to East New Jersey in 1685. Clan Leslie.

LEWIS. Probably a patronymic. John Lewis, from Edinburgh, was in Boston by 1762.

LIDDELL, LIDDLE. Territorial, derived from Liddel in Roxburghshire. A surname in Scotland since the thirteenth century, and later in Ulster. George Liddle settled in Friendsborough, Georgia, in 1775, and Beattie Liddell was transported to the colonies in 1695.

LIMEBURNER. A rare occupational surname used, originally, to describe someone who burnt limestone to produce lime. Early examples date from Glasgow in the sixteenth century. Matthew Limburner, a farmer, emigrated to Boston in 1768.

LINAY. Territorial, derived from the lands of Linay in the Orkney Islands. Examples date back to the sixteenth century there. John Linay and his family from Orkney settled in Richmond County, Georgia, in 1775.

LINDSAY. Territorial, derived either from Normandy or from Lincolnshire, England, and brought to Scotland in the twelfth century. John Lindsay, a merchant from Fife, died in Albany, New York, in 1751, and Reverend David Lindsay settled in Northumberland County, Virginia, around 1645. Clan Lindsay.

LINKLETTER. An Orkney surname of territorial origin dating from the fifteenth century. Alexander Linkletter, a Loyalist in Boston, settled in Nova Scotia in 1783. Clan Sinclair.

LINN. Possibly from the Gaelic word *'linne'* meaning 'pool' or the British word *'llyn'* also meaning pool. George Linn was indentured in Philadelphia in 1697, and William Linn, from Galloway, emigrated to New York in 1774.

LINNING, LINNEN. Examples date from the seventeenth century. Elizabeth Lining was kidnapped and shipped to Charleston in 1684.

LINTRON. Origins unclear, possibly a variant of 'Lendrum' (see above). Found as *'Lentron'* in and around St Andrews. Janet Lintron, a Covenanter, was transported to East New Jersey in 1685.

LISK, LEASK. Territorial, derived from the lands of Leask in Aberdeenshire. Used as a surname since the fourteenth century largely in Aberdeenshire and Orkney. Adam Lisk, from the Shetland Islands, emigrated to Antigua in 1774, and John Lisk from Orkney was in Boston by 1755.

LITHGOW. Territorial, an abbreviation taken from the name of the burgh of Linlithgow. The abridged form has been used since the fourteenth century. Robert Lithgow settled in Glynn County, South Carolina, in 1775.

LITSTER, LISTER, LESTER. Occupational, derived from the Old English term *'littester'* meaning dyer. Used as a surname in Scotland since the thirteenth century. Francis Lester, a hairdresser from Edinburgh, emigrated to Philadelphia in 1774

LITTLE. A descriptive surname used in Scotland since the fourteenth century. The Littles were among the reivers of the Borders, some of whom settled in County Fermanagh during the seventeenth century. Margaret Little was transported to Virginia in 1696, and Andrew Little settled in Antigua in 1725.

LITTLEJOHN. A surname used in Scotland since the fifteenth century. Duncan Littlejohn, a wright from Breadalbane, settled in New York in 1775, and William Littlejohn settled in Edenton, North Carolina, around 1760.

LIVINGSTON. Territorial, derived from the lands of Livingston in West Lothian. An Old English placename signifying the *'ton'* or 'settlement' of *'Leofwine'*, dating from the twelfth century. Used as a surname in Scotland since the thirteenth century, and later in Ireland. Some Livingstones are in fact MacLeays of Appin who adopted the name when assimilating. Robert Livingston [1654-1728] was a merchant and public official in New York, and William Livingstone was transported to East New Jersey in 1685.

LOCH. Probably descriptive, based on the Gaelic word for a 'lake', indicating a place of residence. Early examples date from the thirteenth century and mainly come from south east Scotland. William Loch from Edinburgh emigrated to Jamaica by 1766.

LOCHHEAD. Descriptive, indicating a place of residence at the 'head of the loch or lake'. Early examples come from southern Scotland and date from the thirteenth century. Henry Lochhead, a merchant from Glasgow, settled in Petersburg, Virginia, in 1769, and Hugh Lochhead emigrated to New York in 1775.

LOCKHART. Originally *'Locard'* the surname of a Flemish family that settled in Lanarkshire during the twelfth century. George Lockhart, a surgeon, died in New York in 1698, and Penelope Lockhart was transported to the American Plantations in 1696.

LOGAN. Territorial, derived from a place in Ayrshire, based on the Gaelic word *'lagan'* meaning 'a little hollow'. Examples date from the early thirteenth century in Scotland and later in Ulster. George Logan was a merchant in Princess Anne County, Virginia, before 1781, Walter Logan was the Customs Controller of Perth Amboy, New Jersey, in 1776, and James Logan emigrated from Ulster to Philadelphia by 1769. Clan Logan.

LORIMER. Occupational, being the title of the smith who made all the various pieces of horse-furniture, such as spurs and bits. Examples date from the fifteenth century. Hugh Lorimer emigrated to New York in 1775, and David Lorimer was in Boston by 1749.

LORRAIN. A territorial surname derived from Lorraine in France, and used as a surname since the thirteenth century. W. Lorrain settled in New Hampshire about 1775.

LOTHIAN. Territorial, examples date back to the fifteenth century. John Lothian, who sailed to Darien in 1698, was admitted as a member of the Scots Charitable Society of Boston in 1699.

LOUDEN, LOUDOUN, LOWDEN. Territorial, derived from Loudoun in Ayrshire. Used as a surname since the fifteenth century, James Louden, a Jacobite, was deported to the American colonies in 1747. Clan Campbell.

LOUTTIT. Territorial, derived from a place in Normandy, introduced into Scotland in the twelfth century. Thomas Louttit emigrated to Georgia and settled in Richmond County by 1774.

LOVE. Descriptive, derived from the Old French word *'love'* meaning 'wolf', used a a surname since the fifteenth century. Many of the early examples come from Renfrewshire, also found in Ulster. Reverend David Love settled in Maryland in 1764, and Robert Love enlisted in the Pennsylvania Regiment in 1758.

LOVELL. A Norman-French surname found in Roxburghshire and Angus since the thirteenth century. Ebenezer Lovell was a merchant in Boston around 1752.

LOW. Possibly a Dutch or Flemish surname *'Louw'* meaning 'lion'. Early examples date from the fourteenth century. Alexander Low emigrated from Glasgow to New York in 1774, and John Low, a tailor from Donaghadee, emigrated to Philadelphia, also in 1774.

LUGTON. Territorial, derived from the barony of Lugton in Midlothian. Possibly based on the British *'ilug din'* meaning 'bright hill'. A rare surname with a few examples dating from the sixteenth century. Simon Lugton, a Jacobite from Edinburgh, was transported to the American colonies in 1748.

LUKE. Patronymic, a diminutive of Lucas. A surname in Scotland since the sixteenth century especially in the neighbourhood of Glasgow. William Luke, a merchant in Glasgow, sailed to the West Indies in 1684. Clan Lamont.

LUMSDEN. Territorial, derived from the lands of Lumsden in Berwickshire. Probably Old English with the suffix *'den'* meaning 'valley'. One of the earliest Scottish surnames which dates from the eleventh century. Henry Lumsden, a Jacobite, was deported to Maryland in 1747, while James Lumsden, a baker, emigrated to Virginia in 1774.

LUNAN. Territorial, derived from the barony of Lunan in Angus, Most early examples come from north east Scotland and date from the fourteenth century. Reverend Patrick Lunan settled in Virginia during 1760, and Alexander Lunan, a merchant in Philadelphia, died there in 1770.

LUNDIE. Territorial, derived from the lands of Lundie near Dundee. Possibly based on the Gaelic words *'lon dubh'* meaning 'dark marsh'. Examples of the surname date from the fourteenth century. Archibald Lundie, a merchant from Edinburgh, emigrated to Georgia in 1775, and Reverend James Lundie emigrated to Virginia in 1767.

LYAL, LYLE. Either (a) Descriptive, derived from the French *'de L'isle'* meaning 'of the island', or (b) Patronymic, from the Old English personal name *'Liulf'*.. A surname recorded in Scotland since the twelfth century. David Lyell was in New York by 1701, and a David Lyle settled in New York in 1775.

LYMBURNER. Occupational, derived from the job of burning limestone to produce lime. Most examples come from around Glasgow and date from the sixteenth century. Adam Lymburner, a merchant, settled in Quebec after 1766.

LYON. The surname, which may be English in origin, first appears in Scottish records during the fourteenth century. James Lyon settled in Barbados before 1676, and William Lyon, a Jacobite, was deported to Virginia in 1716. Clan Lyon or Clan Farquharson.

MacADAM From *'MacAdaim'* Gaelic for 'the son of Adam'. Used as a surname in Scotland since the fifteenth century. Archibald McAdam was transported to New England in 1685, while Gilbert McAdam, was transported to Charleston in 1684.

MacALESTER, McALLISTER. From *'MacAlasdair'* Gaelic for 'son of Alexander'. Used as a surname since the fifteenth century in Scotland and in Ulster. John MacAllister was transported to Boston in 1652, Coll McAlester from Kintyre, settled in North Carolina in 1774

MacALLAN. From *'MacAlein'* Gaelic for 'son of Allan'. Used as a surname in Scotland since the fourteenth century and in Ulster from the sixteenth century. John McAllan, a farmer from Argyll, emigrated to New York in 1775

MacALPINE. From *'MacAilpein'* Gaelic for 'son of Ailpean'. Used as a surname since the thirteenth century. Peter McAlpin, from Inverness, settled in New York in 1774, Colin McAlpine, from Edinburgh, died in South Carolina by 1772..

MacANDREW. From *'MacAindreis'* Gaelic for 'son of Andrew'. Used as a surname since the fifteenth century. Alexander McAndrew emigrated to Georgia in 1775.

MacARTHUR. From *'MacArtair'* Gaelic for 'son of Arthur'. Used as a surname since the fourteenth century. John McArthur was the Deputy Governor of St Kitts around 1700, Duncan McArthur emigrated from Jura to Cape Fear in 1754

MacASKELL. From *'MacAsgaill'* a west Highland surname which is partly Gaelic and partly Norse. Used as a surname since the sixteenth century. Allan McAskell died in Barbados before 1702, several McCaskills from Skye settled in North Carolina before the American Revolution

MacAULAY. From *'MacAmhalghaidh'* Gaelic for 'son of Amalghaidh', a branch of Clan Alpine, or from *'MacAmhlaidh'* Gaelic for 'son of Amlaib' a name with a Norse origin and originating in the Hebrides. Recorded as a surname since the thirteenth century. Kenneth McAulay emigrated from Stornaway to Philadelphia in 1774, and Malcolm McAulay, from Argyll, was transported to Jamaica in 1685

MacBAIN. From *'Mac a' ghille bain'* Gaelic for 'son of the fair servant'. A rare surname sometimes confused with McBean. Four Jacobite McBains were transported to the American colonies in 1747.

MacBEAN. From *'Macbheathain'* Gaelic for 'son of Beathain'. Examples date from the sixteenth century. Several Jacobite McBeans were transported to the American colonies in 1716.

MacBEATH, MacBETH. From *'Macbeatha'* Gaelic for 'son of life'. Used since the eleventh century. James McBeth emigrated to Antigua in 1731, and John McBeath was bound for North Carolina in 1774.

MacBRAINE. From *'Mac a' Bhriuthainn'* Gaelic meaning 'son of the judge'. Used as a surname since the sixteenth century. Lachlan McBrayne, a Jacobite, was transported to South Carolina in 1716, and Murdoch McBraine settled in Bladen County, North Carolina, in 1740.

MacBRIDE. From *'Mac Gille Brighde'* Gaelic for 'son of the servant of Bride'. Examples date from the fourteenth century. Hugh and William McBryde, from Ayrshire, were merchants in Maryland before the American Revolution, and Alexander McBryde settled in Moore County, North Carolina, in 1775.

MacBURNIE, MacBIRNIE. A surname from the Gaelic *'MacBiorna'* equivalent to 'son of Bjorn/the bear', found in Dumfries and Galloway since the fifteenth century and later in Ulster. Robert and William McBurnie, from Kirkcudbrightshire, emigrated to Prince Edward Island in 1775.

MacCALL, McCAUL. From *'MacCathail'* Gaelic meaning 'son of Cathal'. Found in south west Scotland since around 1500. James McCall, from Glasgow, settled in Essex County, Virginia, before 1765, George McCall died in Philadelphia in 1740.

MacCALLUM. From *'MacGhilleChaluim'* Gaelic meaning 'son of the servant of Calum'. Duncan McCallum was transported to New England in 1685, Hugh McCallum emigrated to New York in 1775

MacCALMAN. From *'MacCalmain'* Gaelic meaning 'son of Calman'. William McCalman was transported to East New Jersey in 1685.

MacCANN. From *'MacAnna'*, Gaelic meaning 'son of Annadh'. William McCann and his family from Galloway emigrated to New York in 1775.

MacCASKILL. An Anglicisation of the Gaelic surname *'MacAsgaill'* meaning 'son of Askell' a personal name of Norse origin. Several McCaskills from Skye settled in North Carolina before 1775

MacCHISHOLM. A very unusual surname which was possibly a variant of the Gaelic surname *'MacCoiseam'*. John McChisholm, a Covenanter, was transported to Carolina in 1684.

MacCLASER. Possibly derived from the Gaelic surname *'Mac Clarsier'*, an occupational one meaning 'son of the harper'. Alexander MacClaser, a Jacobite, was transported to Montserrat in 1716.

MacCLINTOCK. Originally a Gaelic surname *'Mac Ghill Fhionndaig'* which means 'son of the servant of Fillan', recorded since around 1500 AD. William McClintock, from Glasgow, was in Boston by 1758.

MacCLUMPHA. From *'Mac Gille Iomchadha'* Gaelic meaning 'son of the servant of [Saint] Imchad'. An unusual surname found in Dumfries and Galloway since around 1400. Thomas McClumpha, a farmer from Galloway, emigrated to New York in 1774.

MacCLURG. From *'Mac Luirg'* Gaelic meaning 'son of Lurg'. An unusual surname found in south west Scotland since the thirteenth century. Margaret McClurg, a Covenanter, was banished to the American Plantations in 1684.

MacCOLE, MacCOLL. From *'Mac Colla'* Gaelic meaning 'son of Coll'. A surname traditionally linked with Argyll. McColes from Breadalbane and Glen Orchy emigrated to North Carolina in 1775.

MacCOMB, MacCOLM, MacCOMIE. From *'Mac Thom'* Gaelic meaning 'son of Tom'. Examples date from the sixteenth century. Alexander McComb emigrated from Glen Luce to New York in 1774. Two 'Mackhomes' were transported by Oliver Cromwell to Boston in 1652.

MacCONACHIE. From *'Mac Dhonnchaidh'* Gaelic meaning 'son of Duncan'. Examples of the surname date back to the sixteenth century. Dugall McConachie was banished to the American

Plantations in 1684, Reverend William McConachie died in
Portobacco, Maryland, in 1742

MacCONNELL. From *'Mac Dhomnuill'* Gaelic meaning 'son of
Donald'. A surname traditionally found in Argyll and Galloway.
James McConnell was transported to the American colonies in 1717

MacCORKIE, MacCORKLE. Abbreviations of the Gaelic surname
'MacCorcadail' meaning 'son of Thor's kettle'. Alexander
McCorkie settled in Pennsylvania and later in North Carolina. Clan
Gunn.

MacCORMICK. From *'Mac Cormaig'* Gaelic meaning 'son of Cormac'.
Examples of the surname date back to the medieval period. Mark
and Robert McCormack, Jacobites from Inverness-shire, were
transported to the West Indies in 1747, and James McCormick was
an Irish indentured servant in Pennsylvania during 1771.

MacCORQUDALE. An Anglicisation of the Gaelic surname
'MacCorcadail' meaning 'son of Thor's kettle' implying a partly
Norse origin. A surname recorded since the fifteenth century. Some
claim allegiance to the Clan McLeod.

MacCOULL. A variation of McDougall from the Gaelic name
'MacDhughaill' (see below). A surname recorded since the
fifteenth century. Agnes McCoull, from Perthshire, was banished to
the American Colonies in 1752, and Alexander MacCoull emigrated
to Georgia in 1735. Clan McDougall.

MacCOWAN. From *'MacIlchomhghain'* Gaelic meaning 'son of the
servant of [Saint] Comgan'. Examples of this surname date back to
the medieval period. William McCowan, a Jacobite, was
transported to Maryland in 1747. Clan Colquhoun or Clan Donald
or Clan McDougall.

MacCOY. A variant of McKay, (see below), found mainly in Ulster since
the sixteenth century where it was taken by the gallowglasses from
Argyll. Several Jacobites of that name were transported to the
American colonies in 1716. Clan Donald.

MacCRACKEN. A surname long associated with Galloway but of
unclear origins but possibly derived from MacNaughton. Examples
date back to the early sixteenth century in Scotland and later in
Ulster. John McCracken was in Pennsylvania by 1768 and later in
Rowan County, North Carolina, and John McCracken, from
Galloway, died in Newhaven, Connecticut, by 1769.

MacCRAINE, McCRAN. From *'Mac Crain'* Gaelic meaning 'son of the pig'. Historically localised in the islands of Jura and Islay, Argyllshire. Archibald McCrainie, emigrated from Jura to Cape Fear, North Carolina, in 1754, and Ann McCran, emigrated from Stornaway to New York in 1774.

MacCRAINKEIN. Possibly from the Gaelic *'MacFhraingein'*, or 'son of Frank'(?) John McCrainkein emigrated from Jura to Cape Fear, North Carolina, in 1754.

MacCRAITH, McCREATH. From *'Macrath'* meaning 'son of grace'. A variant of McRae found in south west Scotland from the fifteenth century. John McCreath, from Ayrshire, was transported to the American colonies in 1748, Patrick Mackreith, a prisoner of war, was shipped to Boston in 1652..

MacCREADY, McCREDDIE. A surname associated with Galloway but of unknown origins. John McCready, a blacksmith from Wigtownshire, settled in New York by 1774, and Jane McCreddie was also in New York in 1774.

MacCRINNEL. From *'Mac Raonuill'* meaning 'son of Ronald'. Found as McCrindle, McCrinnel, etc in south west Scotland since the fifteenth century. William McCrinnel, a Scot, served in the Pennsylvania Regiment from 1746.

MacCRORY. From *'Mac Ruadhri'* meaning 'son of the red king'. Examples date from the sixteenth century. Alister Mackrore was transported to Boston by Cromwell in 1652

MacCROW. A variant of MacRae, (see below). Patrick Mackroe settled in Virginia by 1653

MacCUBBIN. A surname traditionally linked with Dumfries and Galloway since the fourteenth century. Probably a variant of MacGibbon. John MacCubbin settled in Anne Arundel County, Maryland, by 1659.

MacCUEAN, MacCUN. From *'MacEoghain'* Gaelic, meaning 'son of Ewen', a surname from Galloway. Walter McCuean was a Covenanter transported to the American colonies in 1685, and William McCunn, from Glasgow, was in Boston by 1743.

MacCULLOCH, MacCULLIE. From *'Mac Chullach'* Gaelic, meaning 'son of the boar', a surname from Galloway dating from the thirteenth century. Anthony McCulloch died in Maryland during 1770, William McCulloch settled in Friendsborough, Georgia, in

1775, and John McCullough emigrated from Belfast to Philadelphia in 1771. Some McCullochs are linked with Clan MacDougall, others with Clan Munro and the rest with Clan Ross.

MacCUMMING. Possibly a variant of the Gaelic surname *'MacCalmain'*. John McCumming was banished to the American Plantations in 1685. Clan Buchanan.

MacCURRIE. A variant of *'MacVurich'* (see below). Andrew McCurrie settled in Georgia by 1761.

MacDANIEL. A variant of MacDonald or MacDonnell, found in Ireland and in Scotland. Daniel McDaniel, a Jacobite from Perth, was transported to the Chesapeake in 1747, and Michael McDaniel was an Irish servant in Cecil County, Maryland, in 1774. Clan Donald.

MacDERMOD, McDERMOTT, McDIARMID. From *'Mac Dhiarmaid'* Gaelic meaning 'son of Dermid'. Examples date back to the fifteenth century. McDiarmids from Breadalbane, Perthshire, emigrated to New York in 1775, while some Jacobite McDermotts were transported to the American colonies in 1716. Clan Campbell.

MacDICHMAYE. An obscure surname of unknown origin. Walter McDichmaye was transported to the American Plantations in 1679.

MacDONALD, MacDONNELL. From *'Mac Dhomhnuill'* Gaelic, meaning 'son of Donald'. The surname has a number of variants with examples dating back to the thirteenth century. A considerable number of McDonalds were banished to the American colonies in 1716 and 1747 after the failure of the Jacobite rebellions. Clan Donald.

MacDONOUGH. An Anglicisation of the Gaelic surname *'MacDonnchaidh'* meaning 'son of Duncan'. John McDonough, a Jacobite from Barra, was transported to the American colonies in 1747, and Mathew MacDonough died in the Danish West Indies in 1762. Clan Robertson.

MacDORTON. A very obscure surname possibly derived from the Gaelic surname *'MacPartlain'* and thus connected with Clan MacFarlane. Philip McDorton, a Jacobite, was transported to Montserrat in 1716.

MacDOUGALL, McDOUGALD. From *Mac Dhughaill'* Gaelic, meaning 'son of Dougal' ie 'son of the dark stranger'. Examples date back to the thirteenth century. William MacDougald, a merchant from Edinburgh, died in East Florida during 1774, while a number of Jacobite and Covenanters named McDougall were banished to the American colonies. Clan MacDougall.

MacDOWELL, McDOUAL. Variants of MacDougall found in Galloway since the thirteenth century and later in Ulster. Alexander McDowall emigrated from Stranraer to New York in 1774. Clan MacDougall.

MacDUFFIE. From *'Mac Duibhshithe'* Gaelic, meaning 'son of the dark man of peace' Variants include McFie and McPhee. Traditionally associated with the island of Colonsay. Examples date from the fifteenth century. John McDuffie, a horsethief from Argyll was exiled to the American colonies in 1732. Clan MacPhee.

MacEACHERN. Derived from the Gaelic surname *'Mac Each-thigh-earna'* which equates 'son of the horse-lord'. The surname can be traced back to the fifteenth century in Argyll. Mary McEachern, born 1740, settled in Scotland County, North Carolina.

MacEACHIN. From *'Mac Eachainn'* Gaelic, meaning 'son of Eachan'. Examples date back to the twelfth century. Patrick McEachin, a blacksmith, settled in North Carolina before 1776.

MacENREE, McHENRY. From *'Mac Eanruig'*, Gaelic meaning 'son of Henry'. Examples date from the fourteenth century. John McEnree moved from Barbados to Virginia in 1679, and James McHenry emigrated from Belfast to Philadelphia in 1771

MacEWAN. From *'Mac Eoghainn'* Gaelic, meaning 'son of Ewan'. Examples date back to the twelfth century. Katherine McEwan, a Jacobite from Fort William was transported to the Chesapeake in 1747. Clan MacLachlan.

MacFADYEN, McFADZEAN, McFADINE. From *'MacPhaidein'* Gaelic, meaning 'son of little Patrick'. Examples date from around 1300 AD. Daniel McFadyen, a lorimer from Glasgow, died in New York during 1781, and Donald McFaiden emigrated to New York in 1775. MacLaine of Lochbuie.

MacFARLANE, McFARLAND. From *'Mac Pharlain'* Gaelic, meaning 'son of Parlan'. Examples date from the fourteenth century. Alexander McFarlane was a tobacco factor in Chaptico, Maryland, by 1761, and Elizabeth McFarlane, a Jacobite banished to the West Indies, landed on Martinique in 1747. Clan MacFarlane.

MacFARQUHAR. From *'Mac Fearchar'* Gaelic, meaning 'son of Farquhar'. Used as a surname since the twelfth century. Reverend

Colin McFarquhar was a minister in Applecross, Pennsylvania, around 1760. Clan Farquharson.

MacFEARGHUIS. Gaelic meaning 'son of Fergus', a surname since the fourteenth century. Roderick MacFearghuis, a Jacobite, was transported to Maryland in 1747. Clan Ferguson.

MacFEE, McFIE, McPHEE. Variants of MacDuffie, (see above). Archibald McFee, a shoemaker from Banff, emigrated to Philadelphia in 1774. and Daniel McPhee, a joiner from Glasgow, emigrated to Maryland in 1775. Clan McPhee.

MacGACHEY, MCGEACHY. An Anglicised version of the Gaelic name 'Mac Eachaidh'. A surname in both Ulster and Scotland. William MacGaheye settled in York, Virginia, by 1653, and Alexander McGeachy, from Argyll, emigrated to America around 1783.

MacGACHIN. Variant of MacEachin, see above. James McGachin, a Covenanter, was banished to Carolina in 1684. Clan MacDougall.

MacGEORGE. A variant of the Ayrshire surname 'MacJarrow'. John McGeorge, from Galloway, emigrated to Prince Edward Island in 1775.

MacGIBBON. Meaning 'son of Gibbon', a surname in use since the fifteenth century. Peter McGibbon emigrated to New York or Georgia in 1775. Clan Campbell or Clan Buchanan.

MacGIE, McGEE, McGHIE. From 'Mac Aodh' Gaelic, meaning 'son of Aodh'. A surname traditionally associated with Dumfries and Galloway in south west Scotland since the thirteenth century. Jean McGie, a Covenanter, was transported to East New Jersey in 1685 while Hugh McGhie, a highwayman, was banished to the American colonies in 1750.

MacGILCHRIST. From 'Mac IlleChriosd' Gaelic, meaning 'son of the servant of Christ', a surname in use since the thirteenth century. Reverend Andrew McGilchrist went to South Carolina in 1741, and Malcolm McGilchrist settled in North Carolina before 1771. Clan Ogilvy or Clan MacLachlan.

MacGILL. From 'Mac an ghoill' Gaelic, meaning 'son of the stranger'. Examples date back to the thirteenth century. James McGill, from Glasgow, became a fur-trader in Quebec by 1776, and Janet McGill was transported to Virginia in 1772.

MacGILLIS, MacGILLIES, MacGILLICH. From *'Mac Gill' Iosa'* Gaelic, meaning 'son of the servant of Jesus', a surname recorded since the twelfth century. Several McGillies's were transported to the West Indies as rebels in 1685 and 1747.

MacGILLVRAY, McGILLIVRAY. From *'Mac Gille brath'* Gaelic, meaning 'son of the servant of doom'. Several Jacobites of the name were transported to South Carolina and the Chesapeake in 1716. Clan McGillivray.

MacGIVEN. Possibly a variant of *'MacIlvain'* from the Gaelic *'Mac Gille Bheathain'* meaning 'son of the servant of Bean'. Alexander McGiven, a Jacobite, was transported to Virginia in 1716. Clan McBean.

MacGLASHAN. From *'Mac Glaisen'* a diminutive of *'McGhille ghlais'* Gaelic, meaning 'son of the grey servant'. Examples date from around 1500. John and Margaret McGlashan were transported to Virginia in 1696.

MacGLON. From *'Mac Giolla Eoin'* Gaelic, meaning 'son of the servant of (Saint) John' thus a variant of McLean. Clan McLean.

MacGOUGHTRY. Possibly from *'Mac Clochaire'* Gaelic, meaning 'son of the mason' a surname found in Galloway. A family of McGoughtries from Kirkcudbrightshire settled in New York in 1774.

MacGOWAN. From *'Mac Ghobhainn'* Gaelic, meaning 'son of the smith', a surname in use since around 1500. Margaret McGowan, from Stirling, emigrated to New York in 1774. Clan Gow or Clan McPherson.

MacGRATH, MacGRAW. From *'MacRath'*, Gaelic, meaning 'son of grace', a variant of MacRae. Henry McGrath from Edinburgh emigrated to Virginia in 1734 as a husbandman and indentured servant. Clan McRae.

MacGREGOR. From *'MacGriogar'* Gaelic meaning 'son of Gregory'. Several Jacobites bearing the surname McGregor were banished to the American colonies in 1716 and also in 1747. Clan McGregor.

MacGRUTHER. From *'Mac Grudaire'* Gaelic, meaning ' son of the brewer'. Traditionally mostly found in Perthshire. William McGruther, a Jacobite, was transported to Virginia in 1716. Clan McGregor.

MacGUFFOG, MacGUFFIE. Two Gaelic surnames of unknown origin, possibly variants, found in Galloway from the thirteenth century. Grizel McGuffog was banished to the American colonies in 1746. Clan McFie.

MacGUIRE. Derived from the Gaelic *'Mac uidhir'* meaning 'son of the pale faced man'. A surname found in Ulster from the medieval period. In Scotland it is considered as a sept of the Clan MacQuarrie of Ulva. Lauchlane McQuarry McGuire, from Argyll, was a skipper in New York before 1783. Clan MacQuarrie

MacGUMRI. Originally a Gaelic surname *'MacCuimrid'* which was a corruption of the surname Montgomery (see above). Angus McGumri, from the Isle of Lewis, emigrated to Philadelphia in 1774, and Peter MacGomery, from Glasgow, was in Boston by 1748.

MacHAFFIE. An Anglicised version of the Gaelic surname *'Mac Gille Chathbhaidh'* meaning 'son of the servant of Cuthbert'. Traditionally localised in Galloway where examples date from the sixteenth century. John McHaffie, a Covenanter, was banished to the American Plantations in 1684.

MacHAIG, McCAIG. A surname taken from the Gaelic name *'MacThaoig'* meaning 'son of the poet'. Associated with south west Scotland, Argyll, and Ulster. John MacHaig, from Galloway, emigrated to New York in 1774. Clan Farquharson or Clan MacLeod.

MacHARDY. Based on a Gaelic name *'MacChardaidh'* meaning 'son of the sloe'. A surname localised in Aberdeenshire since at least the sixteenth century. John MacHardy, a Jacobite, was transported to Virginia in 1716. Clan Mackintosh.

MacHATTON. A surname originating in the Gaelic *'Mac Gille Chatain'* meaning 'son of the servant of Catan'. Examples date from the fifteenth century. Neil McHatton, a Covenanter, was banished to New England in 1685.

MacHUTCHISON, MacHUTCHEON. An Anglicised version of the Gaelic surname *'MacUisdein'* meaning 'son of Hugh'. The Macdonalds of Sleat are sometimes known as the Clan Uisdein indicating descent from Hugh, the younger son of Alexander the Lord of the Isles. Use of the surname dates from the fifteenth century. Hugh McHutchison, a carpenter from Ayr, emigrated to

Quebec in 1775, and James McCuiston, emigrated to Delaware in 1735. Clan Donald.

MacILCHALLUM. A variant of McCallum, (see above). John McIlchallum, a Covenanter from Argyll, was banished to Jamaica in 1685, and John Dow McIlchallum, a horse-thief from Perthshire, was transported to the American Colonies in 1756. Clan McLeod.

MacILMOON. Possibly a corruption of the Gaelic surname *'Mac Calmain'* meaning 'son of Calman'. Donald McIlmoon, from Argyll, was transported to Jamaica in 1685. Clan Buchanan.

MacILPHEDDAR. Derived from the Gaelic surname *'Mac Gille Pheadair'* meaning 'son of the servant of Peter'. A rare surname found in Argyll. Clan McGregor.

MacILRIACH. Based on the Gaelic surname *'Mac gille riabhaich'*, meaning 'son of the bridled lad'. In use 1300 as a surname since around 1300. A group of McIlriachs from Jura emigrated to North Carolina in 1754.

MacILROY. A modification of the Gaelic surname *'Mac ghille ruiadh'*, meaning 'son of the red-haired servant'. A surname since the fourteenth century. Gilbert McIlroy, a Covenanter, was exiled to Jamaica in 1685. Clan Grant.

MacILSHALLUM. A version of the Gaelic surname *'Mac Gille Chaluim'* alias 'son of the servant of Calum', recorded since the fifteenth century. John McIllshallum was transported to Jamaica in 1685. Clan McLeod.

MacILVAINE. A variation of MacGilvane (see MacGivan above). Archibald McIlvain, from Argyll, was transported to Jamaica in 1685. Clan McBain.

MacILVAY. Possibly a variant of Mackelvie, a surname derived from the Gaelic surname *'Mac Shealbhaigh'* meaning 'son of Sealbach'. A surname from Dumfries and Galloway. Duncan McIlvay was transported to Carolina in 1684.

MacILVERRAN. Possibly a version of *'Mac Gille Varquhane'* meaning 'son of the servant of Barchan', recorded since the sixteenth century. Donald McIlverran, a rebel from Argyll, was banished to Jamaica in 1685.

MacILVORY. Either from the Gaelic surname *'Mac Gille Iamhair'* meaning 'son of the servant of Ivor', or a variant of McGillevray (see above). Duncan and John McIlvory, both Covenanters from

Argyll, were transported to the American Plantations in 1685. Clan MacLaine of Lochbuie.

MacINDEORA. Probably derived from the Gaelic surname *'Macindeor'* meaning 'son of Dewar'. A rare surname found in Argyll since the sixteenth century.

MacINNES. A surname originally *'MacAonghuis'*, which is Gaelic for 'son of Angus'. Examples date from the sixteenth century. Malcolm McInnes and his family from Perthshire settled in North Carolina in 1775, and Archibald McInnis, a Jacobite, was exiled to the Chesapeake in 1747. Clan Innes.

MacINTAGGART. This is based on the Gaelic *Mac an t sagairt'* meaning 'son of the priest'. Examples date from the twelfth century. James McTaggart emigrated to New York in 1774. Clan Ross.

MacINTAYLOR. A Gaelic surname of occupational origin as *'Mac an tailleur'* means 'son of the tailor'. Used as early as the fourteenth century. Donald McTaillior, from Perthshire, was banished to Jamaica in 1685.

MacINTOSH. Derived from the Gaelic *'Mac an toisich'* which means 'son of the leader' and used as a surname since the fourteenth century. Several McIntoshes were transported to the American colonies after the failure of the Jacobites in 1716 and 1747. Clan MacIntosh.

MacINTYRE. A Gaelic surname of occupational origin as *'Mac an t saoir'* means 'son of the wright', a name used since the fourteenth century. A number of Jacobites named McIntyre were transported to the American colonies in 1716 and in 1747.

MacISAAC. A patronymic based on the Gaelic surname *'Mac Iosaig'* meaning 'son of Isaac', and dating from the thirteenth century. Malcolm McIsaac from Breadalbane, emigrated to New York in 1775. Clan Campbell or Clan Donald.

MacIVER, MacIVAR, MacEEVAR. An Anglicisation of the Gaelic surname *'MacIomhair'* or 'son of Ivar'. A surname recorded in Scotland since the thirteenth century, also found in Ulster. Some McIvars were banished to Jamaica in 1685, and in 1774 another group of McIvers emigrated to Philadelphia. Some claim allegiance to the Clan Campbell, others to Clan McKenzie and the rest to Clan Donnachaidh alias Robertson.

MacKAY. In Gaelic this is *MacAoidh'* meaning 'son of Aodh or Hugh'. A surname generally associated with the north of Scotland though originally they had links with Argyll. A common surname in Scotland dating from the fourteenth century, and in Ulster since the sixteenth century. Alexander Mackay, a Cromwellian prisoner of war, landed in Boston in 1652, Melashus Mackay emigrated to Virginia in 1635, and in 1730 Daniel Mackay from Belfast was indentured for service in Jamaica. Clan MacKay.

MacKEAN, MacKAINE, MacSHANE. A modification of the Gaelic surname *'MacIain'* meaning 'son of John'. Used in this form since the fourteenth century. Found in Ulster as McShane. Several Mackeans were captured after the Battle of Worcester and despatched to New England in 1651. Clan Donald.

MacKECHNIE. A variant of McEachern (see above). John McKechnie emigrated in 1755 and died in Maine during 1783, and Daniel McKechney, from Dunbartonshire, settled in St Croix by 1769.

MacKEELS. Possibly a variant of 'MacKail' or in Gaelic *'MacCathail'*, that is 'son of Cathal', a family recorded in Bute since around 1500 AD. Daniel McKeels, a Jacobite, was exiled to South Carolina in 1716.

MacKEITH. A variant of Mackeich originally a Gaelic surname *'MacShitich'* meaning 'son of the wolf'. A surname since the fifteenth century. David McKeith was transported to Boston in 1651.

MacKELLAR. An Anglicisation of the Gaelic surname *'Mac Ealair'* otherwise ''son of Hilary'. Examples date back to the fifteenth century. Angus McKellar, a rebel from Argyll, was transported to New England in 1685. Clan Campbell.

MacKEMIE. A form of MacKimmie originally in Gaelic *'MacShimidh'* which means 'son of Simon'. A surname used since the sixteenth century. Reverend Francis Makemie from County Donegal settled in Maryland.by 1683, and Alexander McKimmie, from Inverness, settled in Georgia during 1736.

MacKENNA, MacKENNY, MACKINNEY. An Anglicisation of the gaelic surname *'MacCionaodha'* or 'son of Cionaodh'. Most early examples come from Galloway and are recorded from the sixteenth century. Some Jacobites named McKenny were transported to the American colonies in 1716.

MacKENZIE. From the Gaelic *'MacCoinnich'* meaning 'son of Coinneach', with examples dating back to the thirteenth century. Anne McKenzie, daughter of the Earl of Cromartie, settled in Charleston in 1761. Several Jacobites named McKenzie were transported to the West Indies in 1747, and a group of McKenzies left Stornaway bound for Philadelphia in 1775. Clan Mackenzie.

MacKIE, MACKIE. A variant of Mackay, (see above). An old Stirlingshire family dating back to the fifteenth century while the Mackies in Galloway date from the sixteenth century, also in Ulster from the seventeenth century. Janet McKie was transported to New York in 1682, and some McKies emigrated from Galloway to New York in 1774.

MacKINLAY. An Anglicisation of the Gaelic surname *'MacFhionghuin'* or 'son of Finlay'. Most early examples come from Highland Perthshire and date from the sixteenth century, in Ulster it occurs from the seventeenth century. John McKinlay emigrated to New York in 1775 while another John McKinlay, a cattle rustler, was banished to the American Plantations in 1705. Clan MacFarlane or Clan Buchanan.

MacKINNEL. A surname first noted in Dunbartonshire around 1250 but mainly associated with Dumfries-shire. Mary McKinnel emigrated from Stranraer to New York in 1775, and John McKinnel was a skipper based in New York before 1784.

MacKINNON. Originally the Gaelic surname *'MacFhionghuin'* or 'son of Fionngon', used as a surname since the fifteenth century. Also found in Ireland. John McKinnon, a farmer from Mull, settled in Georgia during 1775, and Reverend Donald McKinnon, from Sleat, settled in Virginia in 1767. Clan McKinnon.

MacKINVEN. A Gaelic surname found as *'MacIonmhuinn'* in Kintyre since the seventeenth century. Duncan McKinvine, from Argyll, was transported to Virginia in 1733.

MacKIRDY, MacCURDY. From the Gaelic surname *'MacUrardaigh'* meaning 'son of the sea ruler', a surname associated with Bute and Arran since the sixteenth century. James MacKirdy, a farmer from Arran, was transported to the American colonies in 1754.

MacKITTERICK. Derived from the Gaelic surname *'MacShitrig'* meaning 'son of Sitrig', a Norse personal name. A surname found

in Galloway since the fourteenth century. John McKitterick, a rioter
from Dumfries, was transported to Maryland in 1771.

MacKNIGHT. (see MacNaught)

MacKRIACH. A very rare name, probably a variant of MacRae, found
in Ayrshire since the fifteenth century. Hugh McKriach emigrated
from Jura to North Carolina in 1754. Clan MacRae.

MacLACHLAN, McLAUGHLIN. From the Gaelic *'MacLachlainn'* or
'son of Lachlan', a surname found in Ireland in the eleventh century
and in Scotland from the thirteenth century. The traditional territory
of the McLachlans is in Cowal, Argyll. Robert McLachlan was a
Cromwellian prisoner of war transported to New England in 1651,
while Thomas and William McLaughlin arrived in Carolina in 1679.
Clan MacLachlan.

MacLAGGAN. Based on the Gaelic surname *'MacGill Adhagain'*
meaning 'son of the servant of Adocan {alias Adomnan}' a surname
recorded since the sixteenth century. John MacLagan emigrated to
Jamaica in 1736. Clan Donnachaidh alias Robertson.

MacLAREN. Originally *'Mac Labhruinn'* a Gaelic surname meaning
'son of Lawrence', a surname in use since the fifteenth century. The
family was mainly centred in Balquhidder, Perthshire. A number of
McLarens, Jacobites, were transported to the colonies in 1716 and in
1747, and others went to North Carolina and New York in 1775.
Clan McLaren.

MacLARTY. A variation of McLaverty based on the Gaelic
'MacFhlaithbheartaich' meaning 'son of the representative', an
agent of the chief. Found in Scotland since the medieval period and
later in Ulster. Alexander McLarty settled in North Carolina in
1773. Clan Donald.

MacLATCHIE. Originally a Gaelic surname *'Mac Gilla Eidich'* or 'son
of the servant of Eidich'. A surname mostly found in Ayrshire from
the sixteenth century. Charles MacLatchie settled in East Florida by
1774, and Robert McLatchie was a schoolmaster in Savannah before
1766

MacLAY, McLEA, McLEAY. Derived from either the Gaelic surname
'Mac Donnsleibhe' meaning 'son of brown of the hill', or *'Mac an
leigh'* meaning 'son of the physician', names found in Scotland and
Ireland. Dougal McLea, a Jacobite, was transported to the colonies

in 1747, and John McLea emigrated to New York in 1775. Some
are linked with Clan Stewart.

MacLEAN, MACLAINE. An Anglicisation of the Gaelic surname *'Mac
Gille Eoin'* meaning 'son of the servant of John'. Examples date
back to the fourteenth century. A number Covenanters named
McLean were transported to the American colonies in 1685, and a
larger number of Jacobites were banished there in 1716 and 1747.
Clans McLean or MacLaine.

MacLEHOSE. A corruption of the Gaelic surname *'Mac Gille
Thamhais'* otherwise 'son of the servant of Thomas'. Recorded in
central Scotland since the fifteenth century. John MacLehose, a
merchant from Glasgow, died in Jamaica during 1782, and Malcolm
MacLehose settled on Cape Fear, North Carolina, in 1770. Clan
Campbell.

MacLEISH, MacLESE. Derived from the Gaelic surname *'MacGill
Iosa'* meaning ' son of the servant of Jesus'. A surname in Scotland
since the fourteenth century, and later in Ulster. Duncan McLeish, a
Jacobite, was transported to the West Indies in 1747. Clan
MacPherson.

MacLELLAN. Originally a Gaelic name *'Mac Gill Fhaolain'* meaning
'son of the servant of Fillan'. Early examples are mostly found in
Galloway and date from the fourteenth century. The MacLellans in
Perthshire claim allegiance to the Clan McNab. Margaret McLelan,
a Covenanter, was transported to East New Jersey in 1685, and
William MacLellan died in Darien in 1698. Clan McLellan.

MacLENNAN. An Anglicisation of the Gaelic surname *'Mac Gill
Fhinnein'* or 'son of the servant of Finnan'. A surname in use since
the thirteenth century. Several Jacobites bearing the name were
transported to Barbados in 1747, while a group of McLennans
emigrated to New York in 1774. Clan MacLennan.

MacLEOD. Derived from the Gaelic surname *Mac Leoid'* meaning 'son
of Leoid' a Norse personal name. Examples of the surname date
back to the thirteenth century. Several McLeods emigrated from
Inverness to Georgia during the 1730s, while John McLeod, a
Royalist soldier, was transported there in 1651. Clan McLeod.

MacLURE. A surname from Galloway where the name is found since the
sixteenth century. In Gaelic it appears as *'Mac Gill uidhir'* which
translates as 'son of the servant of Odhar'. The MacLures of the

western Highlands are said originally to have been *'Mac a leabhair'* or 'devotees of the book'. Also found in Ulster. Anthony MacLure was in Boston by 1724, and John McLure settled in Carolina around 1685. Some McLures are linked to the Clan McLeod.

MacMARTIN, MacMARTINE. A corruption of the Gaelic *'MacMhartainn'* or 'son of Martin', a surname since the thirteenth century. Several McMartins from Breadalbane settled in New York in 1775. Clan Cameron or Clan Donald.

MacMASTER. Originally *'Mac a' Mhaighstir'* which means 'son of the master', a surname found mainly in Dumfries and Galloway since the fifteenth century. James and John McMaster, merchants, settled in Boston in 1766, and a group of McMasters emigrated from Stranraer to New York in 1774. Clan Buchanan.

MacMATH. Based on a Gaelic surname *'Mac Mhatha'* or 'son of Matthew', a name recorded since the fifteenth century. John McMath in New England in 1741, and John McMith in Boston by 1711. Clan Matheson.

MacMEEKAN, McMIKAN, McMEEKING. Other surnames from Galloway which were originally in Gaelic as *'MacMiadhachain'*, or 'son of the honoured one'. Recorded since the twelfth century. Also found in Ulster. Several McMickens from Galloway emigrated to New York in 1774 and 1775.

MacMICHAEL. Derived from *'McMicheil'*, Gaelic for 'son of Michael' and recorded since the early thirteenth century. Duncan and Roger McMichael, rebels, were transported to Jamaica in 1685.

MacMILLAN. In Gaelic this appears as *'MacMhaolain'* which means 'son of the bald one', a surname since the thirteenth century. Also recorded in Ulster since the Plantation. Alister McMillan settled in Salem, Massachusetts, by 1661, and Donald McMillan, from Islay, emigrated to New York in 1739. Clan McMillan.

MacMORRAN. Originating in the Gaelic surname *'MacMughron'* which in English is 'son of the seal's slave'. Examples date back to the fourteenth century. Edward McMorran, a merchant from Dumfries, emigrated to New York in 1774, and John McMoran was in Boston by 1693. Clan McKinnon.

MacMUNN. An Anglicised form of *'Mac Gille Mhunna'* or in English 'son of the servant of Munn', a surname since the thirteenth century. George McMin was in Boston by 1727.

MacMURCHIE. Derived from the Gaelic surname *'MacMhurchaidh'* which means 'son of Murdoch', recorded since the thirteenth century. Some McMurchie families from Kintyre settled on Cape Fear, North Carolina, during the early 1770s. Clan Buchanan or Clan Menzies.

MacMURPHY. Originally a Gaelic surname *'MacMurchadha'* or 'son of the sea-warrior' found in Arran, Argyll and Ulster. Archibald McMurphy enlisted in the Pennsylvania Regiment in 1758.

MacMURRAY. A surname found in Galloway since the sixteenth century. originally a Gaelic surname *'MacMuireadhaigh'* or 'son of the navigator. As the name was recorded in medieval Ulster it may have spread to Scotland from there. Alexander McMurray emigrated from Stranraer to New York in 1774. Clan Murray.

MacMURRWICK. Possibly a variant of *'Mac Murrich'* (see Mac Murray above). Alexander MacMurrwick emigrated from Inverness to Georgia in 1735.

MacNAB, McNABB. From the Gaelic surname *'Mac an Aba'* which means 'son of the abbot'. A surname associated with Highland Perthshire since the medieval period. Donald McNab was a soldier in New York in 1759, while a Mr McNab was recorded in Mobile in 1767. Clan McNab.

MacNAIR. Either for the Gaelic name *'Mac Iain Uidhir'* meaning 'son of sallow John', or from *'Mac an Oighre'* alias 'son of the heir'. Robert McNair, a cooper, emigrated to Darien in 1698.

MacNAMAIL A very rare surname derived from the Gaelic *'Mac na maoile'* or 'son of baldness', Dugald MacNamail from Jura emigrated to Cape Fear, North Carolina, in 1754. Clan MacMillan.

MacNAUGHT, MacKNIGHT, MacNUTT. A surname found in Dumfries and Galloway since the thirteenth century and later in Ulster as McNutt. Possibly a diminutive of MacNaughton. John and Daniel McNaught emigrated from Stranraer to New York in 1774, while Grace McKnaight sailed from Belfast bound for Philadelphia in 1773. Clan McNaughton.

MacNAUGHTON, MCNACHTON. An Anglicisation of the Gaelic surname *'Mac Neachdainn'* meaning 'son of Nechtan', a Pictish king. Examples of the surname date back to the thirteenth century. Several McNaughtons from Breadalbane, Perthshire, emigrated to New York in 1775. Clan MacNaughton.

THE SCOTTISH SURNAMES OF COLONIAL AMERICA

MacNEELAGE. A variant of the Gaelic surname *'MacNiallghuis'* or
'son of Niallghus'. Donald McNeelage, from Argyll, was in New
York by 1759. Clan McNeil or Clan Lamont.

MacNEILL. A Gaelic surname meaning *'son of Neill'* which dates from
the fourteenth century. Also found in Ireland. Archibald McNeill,
from Colonsay, settled in Princess Anne County, Virginia, during
1739, and Neil McNeil was a merchant in St Kitts by 1758, and
Archibald McNeel emigrated from Larne to Charleston in 1773.

MacNEISH, McNISH. A surname based on a Gaelic one *'Macneis'* a
variant of *'MacAonghus'* or 'son of Angus'. Examples of the
surnames date back to the fourteenth century. George MacNish,
from Glasgow, died in New York during 1722, Daniel and Patrick
Macknith were prisoners of war transported to Boston in 1651. Clan
McGregor.

MacNICOL. An Anglicised version of the Gaelic name *'MacNeacail'*
alias 'son of Nicol or Nicholas', a surname found in the west
Highlands and in Angus since the fifteenth century. Nicol McNicol,
was a soldier in Georgia around 1743, and Donald McNicoll was a
tobacco factor in Pittsylvania County, Virginia, by 1760. Some
McNicols are linked to Clan Campbell.

MacNIVEN. Derived from the Gaelic surname *'MacNaoimhin'* meaning
'son of the holy one'. Some McNivens from Islay, settled in New
York in 1738. Certain MacNivens claim allegiance to Clan Comyn,
some to Clan Mackintosh, and others to Clan MacNaughton.

MacOWEN. A variant of McCowan (see above). Agnes McOwen
emigrated from Stranraer to New York in 1774,and Catherine
MacOwin, a Jacobite, was transported to the American colonies in
1747.

MacPHADEN. See McFadyen (above)

MacPHAIL. A Gaelic surname meaning 'son of Paul' which dated from
the fifteenth century. Later it appears in Ulster as 'McFall'. A
group of McPhails from Lewis emigrated to Philadelphia in 1775,
Clan McPhail.

MacPHERSON. An Anglicisation of the Gaelic surname
'MacPhearsain' meaning 'son of the parson'. A surname recorded
since the fifteenth century. Several MacPhersons were banished to
the American colonies for participating in the Jacobite rebellions of

1715 and 1746. Donald McPherson, an apprentice writer from Inverness, settled in Pensacola, West Florida, in 1771.

MacQUARRY. Derived from the Gaelic surname *'MacGuaire'* meaning 'son of the proud one' and dating from the fifteenth century. A surname associated with Mull and Ulva. Five Jacobites bearing the surname McQuarry, all from Eigg, were transported to the West Indies in 1747.

MacQUEEN. An Anglicisation of the Gaelic surname *'Mac Shuibhne'* meaning 'son of Sveinn', implying a Norse origin. James MacQueen emigrated to Georgia in 1735.

MacQUILLAN. An Anglicisation of the Gaelic surname *'Mac Uighilin'* meaning 'son of Hugh'. James McQuelin from County Antrim, emigrated to Maryland in 1720.

MacQUISTON A corruption of the Gaelic surname *'Mac Uisdean'* meaning 'son of Hugh'. Recorded since the seventeenth century in Scotland and in Ulster. Anthony McQueeston emigrated from Stranraer to New York in1775, while John McQuiston also sailed from there to North Carolina in the same year, and David McQuestin left Larne bound for Charleston in 1773. Clan Donald.

MacRAE. Derived from the Gaelic name *Mac rath'* or 'son of grace or prosperity'. A surname recorded in Scotland since the thirteenth century, and later in Ulster. Allan McRae was a merchant in Virginia by 1653, and Reverend Christopher McRae settled in Virginia during 1766. Clan McRae.

MacROB. The Gaelic equivalent of 'son of Rob'. A surname since the fifteenth century. Duncan McRob, a tailor from Kintyre, settled in North Carolina in 1774. Clans Buchanan, Gunn or Innes.

MacROBERT. An Anglicisation of *'Mac Roibeirt'*, or 'son of Robert'. Examples date from the sixteenth century. Reverend Archibald McRoberts went to Virginia in 1761, and Peter McRobert emigrated to New York in 1774. Clan Robertson or Donnachaidh.

MacRORY. Originally a Gaelic surname *'Mac Ruairidh'* or 'son of Rory', recorded since the thirteenth century. Alester MackRore was transported to Boston in 1651.

MacSLIPHEDER. Derived from the Gaelic surname *'Mac Gille Pheadair'* or 'the son of {Saint} Peter'. Recorded in Argyll since the seventeenth century. John McSlipheder emigrated from Jura to Cape Fear in 1754.

MacSPARRAN, MacSPORRAN. An Anglicisation of the Gaelic surname *'Mac an sporain'* translated as 'son of the purse-bearer'. Examples date from the seventeenth century. Reverend James McSparran settled in New England in 1720. Clan Donald.

MacTAGGART. Derived from the Gaelic surname *'Mac an t-sagairt'* or 'son of the priest'. Examples date from as early as the thirteenth century, also found in Ireland. James McTaggart emigrated to New York in 1774, and John McTagard, from Irvine, was in Boston by 1725. Clan Ross.

MacTAILLIOR A Gaelic surname meaning 'son of the taylor' which has been in use since the fourteenth century. Donald McTaillior, a Covenanter from Perthshire, was transported to Jamaica in 1685.

MacTAVISH Originally a Gaelic surname *'Mac Tamhais'* which means 'son of Thomas', a surname found in Argyll since the fourteenth century. Donald McTavish was banished to the American colonies in 1755. Clan Campbell.

MacTHOMAS. An Anglicised version of the Gaelic surname *'MacTomais'* or 'son of Thomas'. Examples date from the sixteenth century mainly in Glen Shee. Alester MacThomas, a prisoner of war, was exiled to New England in 1651. Clan Mackintosh.

MacVEY. Derived from the Gaelic surname *'MacBheatha'*. A surname since around 1500. Donald McVey, a Covenanter, was banished to the American Plantations in 1685. Clan McLean.

MacVIAN, MacVEAN, MacVANE. See MacBean (above). A group of McVians from Breadalbane, Perthshire, settled in New York in 1775. Clan McBean.

MacVICAR. From the Gaelic surname *Mac Bhiocair'* meaning 'son of the vicar'. Used since the fourteenth century. Duncan McVicar, a merchant from Glasgow, settled in Charleston by 1758, and Duncan McVicar, a Covenanter from Argyll, was transported to New England in 1685. Clan McNaughton.

MacVURICH. From the Gaelic surname *'McMhuirich'* meaning 'son of the seafarer'. Examples date from the sixteenth century. Malcolm McVorich was transported to East New Jersey in 1685, and Archibald McUrich, from Argyll, was banished to New England in 1685.

MacWALTER. An Anglicised version of the Gaelic surname *'MacBhaltair'* meaning 'son of Walter'. Examples date from the sixteenth century and generally come from south west Scotland. William McWalter and Thomas Gualter were prisoners of war exiled to New England by Oliver Cromwell in 1650. Clan MacFarlane.

MacWHAE, MacWHA, McQUHAE. Taken from the Gaelic surname *'MacAodha'* meaning 'son of Hugh'. Most early examples come from Wigtownshire. Robert McWhae emigrated from Kirkcudbright to New York in 1775.

MacWHORTER. A version of the Gaelic surname *'Mac Chruitter'* or 'son of the harper' found in Ayrshire. Examples of the name date back to the fourteenth century. Also found in Ulster. John McWhorter, from Ayrshire, was in Boston by 1770. Clan Buchanan.

MacWILLIAM. From the Gaelic surname *'MacUilleim'* meaning 'son of William', and used since the twelfth century. Also found in Ulster. A number of McWilliams from Galloway emigrated to New York in 1774, and Archibald McWilliams emigrated from Larne to Charleston in 1773. Clan Gunn or Clan MacFarlane.

MAIDEN. Possibly territorial from Maden in Lancashire. A very unusual surname in Scotland. William Maiden, from Dundee, died in Philadelphia before 1756.

MAILER. Territorial, derived from the lands of Mailer in Forteviot, Perthshire. Recorded as a surname since the thirteenth century. Andrew Mailer settled in Virginia in 1666.

MAIN, MEAN, MEIN. Probably diminutives of either the Scandinavian *'Magnus'* or the Flemish *'Maynard'*. Those from northern Scotland may well be of Norse origin whereas those from the south probably originate in Flanders. Examples date from the fifteenth century. Joan Main, from Edinburgh, was transported to the American Plantations in 1697, while John Mein, a bookseller from Edinburgh, emigrated to Boston in 1765.

MAIR, MAJOR. An occupational surname, designating a range of office holders. Used as a surname in Scotland since the thirteenth century. Daniel Mair, a Glasgow weaver, emigrated to New York in 1774, and William Main, from Stirling, was transported to East New Jersey in 1685. .

MAITLAND. A surname of uncertain origin which first appears in Scotland in 1227 as *'de Matulant'*. Most examples come from south east Scotland. Rev. John Maitland was sent to Carolina in

1707, while another John Maitland, a Jacobite from County Armagh, was transported to the American colonies in 1747.

MALCOLM. Originally a Gaelic personal name *'Mael Coluimb'* meaning 'devotee of (Saint) Columba', but by the thirteenth century it had become a surname. Reverend Alexander Malcolm settled in Marblehead, Massachusetts, around 1739, and James Malcolm, a merchant, died in Jamaica by 1756. Clan Malcolm.

MALLOCH. A Gaelic descriptive surname indicating *'shaggy eyebrows'*. John Malloch was the skipper of the <u>Endeavour</u> on the Darien Expedition of 1698, and a John Malloch was in Boston by 1706.

MANN. Patronymic, a diminutive of the Norse forename *'Magnus'*. Examples date from the fifteenth century. William Mann, a Jacobite, was exiled to Maryland in 1716, and Rev. Isaac Mann was sent to Dominica in 1774.

MANSON. A patronymic surname of Norse origin meaning *'son of Magnus'*, traditionally associated with Caithness and the Northern Isles. Examples date from the fifteenth century. Some Manson families from Orkney settled in Georgia in 1774. Clan Gunn.

MANUEL. Territorial, derived from the lands of Manuel, originally the Priory of Emanuel, in Stirlingshire. Used as a surname since the thirteenth century. James Manuel, a Covenanter, was transported to the West Indies in 1678.

MARJORYBANKS. Territorial, possibly from the lands of Marjoribanks in West Calder, near Edinburgh. Used as a surname since the sixteenth century. George Marjoribanks, a Jacobite, was exiled to Virginia in 1716, while Thomas Marjoribanks, a baker from Glasgow, emigrated to Philadelphia in 1774.

MARNOCH. A surname of territorial origin derived from the lands of Marnoch in Aberdeenshire. Most early examples come from the north east and date from the fifteenth century. Alexander Marnoch, a Jacobite from Aberdeen, was banished to the West Indies in 1747, and Gilbert Marnock, a Covenanter, was transported there in 1678.

MARR. Territorial, based on the district of that name in Aberdeenshire. Examples date from the thirteenth century. Alexander Marr, a Jacobite, was transported to the Chesapeake in 1747

MARSHALL. An occupational surname of French origin introduced into Scotland by the Anglo-Normans in the twelfth century. The French word *'marechal'* means 'horse- servant' or 'groom'. In Scotland the surname appears as early as 1136. James Marshall, an innkeeper from Aberdeen, died in Charleston in 1765, and Reverend Mungo Marshall was sent to Virginia in 1744.

MARTIN. This forename and later surname has developed directly or indirectly, via Gaelic, from St Martin a popular saint in the Middle Ages. Robert Martin died in Maryland in 1725, while Daniel Martin was transported to New England in 1651.

MASON. A surname of occupational origin based on the French term *'macon'*. Used as a surname in Scotland since the thirteenth century. Reverend John Mason settled in New York by 1765, and Janet Mason was transported to Virginia in 1696.

MASSIE. A Norman-French surname. Lawrence Massie was transported to Virginia in 1696

MASTERTON. Territorial, derived from the lands of Masterton near Dunfermline. Used as a surname since the thirteenth century. Christian Masterton was banished to the American Plantations in 1695.

MATHER. Probably a territorial surname based on the place Mathers near Montrose, though possibly an occupational surname derived from the Old English word *'moedere'* meaning reaper.. Recorded since the sixteenth century. David Mather, a Covenanter, was transported to the American colonies in 1670.

MATHESON, MATHIESON. Patronymic meaning *'son of Matthew'*. Examples of the surname date from the fourteenth century. James Matheson emigrated to North Carolina, and Janet Mathison went to Philadelphia, both in 1775. Clan Matheson.

MATTHEW. From the Biblical forename Matthew which had become a surname in Scotland by the seventeenth century. Two Andrew Matthews, both Jacobites, were transported to the West Indies in 1747.

MAULE. A territorial surname from France introduced by the Anglo-Normans in the twelfth century. The family name of the Earls of Panmure. Relatively uncommon. Reverend James Maull died in Antigua by 1697.

MAVOR, MAWER. An occupational surname derived from the Gaelic word *'maor'* meaning 'a petty office holder'. Most early examples come from the area between Inverness and Aberdeen and date from the sixteenth century. Mark Mavor, a Covenanter from Inverness-shire, was transported to the American colonies in 1685. Clan Innes.

MAXTON. Territorial, taken from Maxton, the 'settlement or tun of Maccus', in Roxburghshire. By the thirteenth century the place-name had become a surname. James Maxton, a forger from Edinburgh, was transported to the American colonies in 1767.

MAXWELL. Territorial, taken from a place-name in Roxburghshire. Maxwell means the 'wiel' or pool of Maccus. Used as a surname since the twelfth century, found mainly in the Borders. Charles Maxwell, a Covenanter from Nithsdale, was banished to the American Plantations in 1684, Rev. William Maxwell emigrated to South Carolina in 1726. Clan Maxwell.

MEARNS. Another surname of territorial origin but one originating from two sites of that name, one near Glasgow and another south of Aberdeen. The name is based on the Gaelic words *'an Mhaoirne'* meaning 'the Stewartry'. Examples of the surname date from around 1400. Elizabeth Mearns, from Aberdeen, was transported to the American colonies in 1773.

MEARSON. A patronymic of unknown origin recorded since the eighteenth century. John Mearson, a wright from Stirling, emigrated to New York in 1775.

MEIKLE, MUCKLE. A descriptive surname based on the old Scots word for 'big' or 'large'. Used since the fifteenth century. Rev. Robert Meikle, a Covenanter, was banished to the West Indies in 1678, Robert Meikle was transported to Maryland in 1772., and Robert Muckle, a Jacobite, was transported to the American colonies in 1747.

MEIKLEJOHN. Another descriptive surname. One which has been in use since the seventeenth century and means 'Big John'. John Meiklejohn, a Jacobite, was transported to Barbados in 1747.

MELDRUM. Territorial, taken from Meldrum, formerly Melgedrum, in Aberdeenshire. A Gaelic placename *'malag druim'* or 'noble ridge'. A surname since the thirteenth century particularly in the north east. Rev. George Meldrum, from Banffshire, was banished to the American Plantations in 1685, and Rev. William Meldrum was sent to Virginia in 1756.

MELLORD. Possibly a variant of 'Millward' meaning a 'mill manager'. David Mellord, from Orkney, emigrated to Georgia in 1775.

MELROSE. Territorial, based on the name of a burgh in Roxburghshire. An uncommon surname, in use since the fifteenth century. William Melrose was in Boston by 1699.

MELVILLE. A Norman surname originating in Malaville, Normandy. First example dates from the twelfth century. David Melville, a merchant from Glasgow, settled in Boston during the 1690s, and William Melville, a Jacobite, was transported to Maryland in 1747.

MELVIN. A variation of Melville dating from the twelfth century. David Melvin was a member of the Scots Charitable Society of Boston in 1692, and James Melvin settled in East New Jersey in 1685.

MENNIE. Territorial, derived from the lands of Mennie in Aberdeenshire. Robert Miny was transported to New England around 1650.

MENZIES. A territorial surname of Norman-French origin, originally '*de Meyners*'. The surname appears in various forms from the thirteenth century onwards in Scotland. Ninian Menzies from Glasgow was a merchant in Richmond, Virginia, before 1776, who died in St Eustatia in 1781, and Alexander Menzies of Cammo, was a judge and advocate in Boston in the late seventeenth century. In Gaelic the surname becomes '*Meinnearech*'. Clan Menzies.

MERCER. A surname of occupational origin taken from '*mercier*' the French word for a 'draper'. Examples date from around 1200 in Scotland. The family is traditionally found in Perthshire. Dr Hugh Mercer, from Aberdeenshire, died at the battle of Princeton in 1777, and James Mercer, a soldier from Perth, died at Oswego during the French and Indian Wars.

MERCHISTON. MERSTON, MESTON. Territorial, based on a place-name near Edinburgh, possibly meaning '*the village of Mark*'. A rare surname with examples dating from the mid-fifteenth century. Robert Merchiston, a surgeon's mate, died in Darien during 1699.

MERRY, MIRRY. Possibly a descriptive surname. Examples date from the seventeenth century. Henry Merry settled in Massachusetts in 1661.

MICHIE. A diminutive of 'Michael' found in Highland Aberdeenshire since the sixteenth century. John Michey, a Jacobite, was transported to Virginia in 1716, and William Michie was a merchant in Charleston before 1772.

MIDDLEMISS, MIDDLEMASS. A territorial surname originating in Roxburghshire and used as a surname since the fifteenth century. Possibly derived from the Middle March of the Scottish Borders. James Middlemiss and his son James, farmers from Roxburghshire, were transported to the American colonies in 1726.

MIDDLETON. A surname of territorial origin taken from the lands of Middleton of Conveth in Laurencekirk. In use as a surname since the thirteenth century especially in the north-east. Dr Peter Middleton died in New York during 1752, while John Middleton emigrated to Philadelphia in 1775. Some Middletons claim to be a sept of the Clan Innes.

MILL. A surname originally indicating a place of residence. Examples date from the sixteenth century. James Mill, an exiled Jacobite, was landed at Port Oxford, Maryland, as an indentured servant on 5 August 1747.

MILLAR, MILLER. An occupational surname, common throughout Scotland since the medieval period. William Millar, a farmer from Orkney, and his family settled in Richmond County, Georgia, in 1775, and Farquhar Millar, a gardener from Edinburgh, was banished as a Jacobite to the Chesapeake in 1747.

MILLIGAN, MILLIKEN, Surnames derived from the Gaelic name *'Maolagan'* meaning 'the little bald one'. Most early examples come from Dumfries and Galloway and date from the thirteenth century. James Milligan, a merchant from Kirkcudbright, settled in Philadelphia by 1772, and a Mr Milliken settled on Nevis before 1700.

MILLWANE. An abbreviation of 'McIlvain'. Examples date from the seventeenth century. Janet Milwain, from Wigtonshire, emigrated to New York in 1775.

MILNE. A surname indicating a place of residence – a mill or milne, a term ultimately from the Latin word *'molina'*. A very common name particularly in north-east Scotland. Card Milne, from Strathbogie, was transported to Virginia in 1669, while Robert Milne died in Curacao in 1714. Some Milnes are associated with the Clan Ogilvy while others with the Clan Gordon.

MILNER. An occupational surname equivalent to 'Miller' which has been used since the fifteenth century. James Milner, from Aberdeenshire, died in North Carolina in 1771.

MILROY. An abbreviation of the surname *'McIlroy'* found in south west Scotland since the seventeenth century. Anthony Milroy, from Galloway, emigrated to New York in 1774.

MILTON. Descriptive indicating a place of residence – *' the ton or settlement by the mill'*. Mary Miltoun was transported to Virginia in 1696.

MITCHELL. A patronymic based on *'Michel'* the French version of 'Michael'. Found as a forename by the fifteenth century in Scotland, and in Ireland, particularly Ulster, at a later date. James Mitchell, from Glasgow, settled in Connecticut around 1730, and several Jacobites bearing the surname Mitchell were transported to the American colonies in 1716 and in 1747. Some Mitchells are linked with the Clan Innes.

MITCHELSON. Another patronymic based derived from Mitchell or Michael. Examples too date back to the fifteenth century. David Mitchelson, from Kirriemuir, was in Boston by 1767.

MOCHLINE. Territorial, derived from Mauchline in Ayrshire, based on the Gaelic term *'magh linne'* meaning 'the plain with the pool'. A very rare surname. William Mochline, from Glasgow, was a planter in Brunswick County, Virginia, by 1749.

MOFFAT. Territorial, derived from Moffat in Dumfries-shire, based on the Gaelic term *'magh fada'* meaning 'the long plain'. Examples date from the early thirteenth century. Jean Moffat, a Covenanter, was transported to East New Jersey in 1685, and around the same time James Moffat was transported to Carolina.

MOIR, MORE, MOORE, MOER. Descriptive surnames based on the Gaelic word *'mor'* meaning 'large'. Examples date from the early fourteenth century. Dr Alexander Moir died in St Croix during 1766, Reverend James Moir died in Edgecombe County, North Carolina, in 1766, and Alexander More, from Kirkwall, settled in Georgia during 1775.

MOLLISON. A patronymic, presumably meaning 'son of Molly'. Recorded in Aberdeen since the sixteenth century. Thomas Molison, a clerk from Brechin, emigrated to Maryland in 1730, and Gilbert Mollison was in Perth Amboy, East New Jersey, by 1699.

MONCREIFF. A name of territorial origin derived from the lands of Moncreiff near Perth. Based on the Gaelic words *'Monadh Croiidh'* signifying 'the hill with the trees'. Examples of the surname date

THE SCOTTISH SURNAMES OF COLONIAL AMERICA

from the thirteenth century. Reverend Robert Moncreiff went to
Antigua in 1748, and George Moncreiff was a shipbuilder in Boston
around 1739.

MONCUR. Another surname of territorial origin derived from lands of
that name in Angus. Based on the Gaelic words *'moine chuir'*
meaning 'the moor with the bend'. A surname in use since the early
thirteenth century particularly in the neighbourhood of Dundee.
James Moncur settled in South Carolina by 1685, and Thomas
Moncur, from Dundee, was in Boston by 1739.

MONORGAN. Territorial, taken from the lands of Monorgund in the
Carse of Gowrie and used as a surname since the thirteenth century
in Angus and Perth. A Gaelic term with the prefix *'moine'* meaning
'moor'. Gilbert Monorgan, a Covenanter, was transported to East
New Jersey in 1685.

MONRO, MONROE, MUNRO. A Gaelic surname, possibly a
placename bearing the prefix 'mun' or *'moine'* meaning moor, in
use since the fourteenth century. William Munro died in
Massachusetts in 1717, and Duncan Monro, a Jacobite transportee,
landed on Martinique in 1747.

MONTEITH, MENTEITH. Territorial, a name taken from the lands of
Monteith in Perthshire and used as a surname since the early
thirteenth century. The name is Gaelic with the prefix *'moine'*
meaning moor, followed by 'Teith' the name of the nearby river,
thus 'the moor by the Teith'. William Monteath, a farmer from
Caithness, emigrated to New York in 1775, and a merchant named
William Monteith settled in Jamaica by 1777

MONTIER. Possibly of French origin with examples in Scotland dating
from the seventeenth century. James Montier, from Glasgow, was in
Boston by 1739.

MONTGOMERY. A surname of territorial origin based on a placename
in Normandy. Introduced into Scotland during the twelfth century.
The family settled initially in Renfrewshire and Ayrshire and from
there to Ulster during the seventeenth century. Hew Montgomery, a
merchant, sailed from Glasgow to Virginia in 1685, William
Montgomery settled in Carolina before 1690, and David
Montgomery emigrated from Larne to Charleston in 1772. Clan
Montgomery.

MONTROSE. Territorial, derived from the burgh of that name in Angus. Bsaed on the Gaelic words *'moine rois'* meaning 'moor on the promontary'. Examples of the surname date from the early thirteenth century. Now a rare surname in Scotland. Laughlin Montrose, a Royalist prisoner of war, was deported to New England in 1652.

MOORE, MORE, MUIR. Either from the English word meaning a moor or heath or from the Gaelic word *'Mohr'* meaning 'great'. A surname dating from the thirteenth century. Anne Moore landed in Boston in 1763, Ann Muir emigrated to Philadelphia in 1775, and Alexander More settled in Georgia in 1775.

MORELAND. Derived from one of a number of places throughout Scotland, William Morland, from Stranraer, was in Boston by 1762.

MORGAN. In Scotland the surname was originally *'Morgund'* but has been standardised in line with the Welsh surname *'Morgan'*. Both are of Celtic origin. Traditionally the surname was associated with Aberdeenshire where it used since the medieval period. Patrick Morgan, a Jacobite from Aberdeenshire, was transported to the Chesapeake in 1747, and Reverend William Morgan settled in Jamaica in 1773.

MORN, MORRIN. Diminutives of the Gaelic surname *'MacMorran'*. Dr Charles Morrin, from Dumfries, settled in Jamaica by 1772, while John Morn, from Orkney, settled in Georgia in 1775.

MORRISON, MORISON. This surname can either be an English patronymic meaning *'son of Morris'* or a Gaelic surname *'Muirgheasain'*. Alexander Morrison, from Skye, died in Carthage, North Carolina, in 1777, and Archibald Morrison was in Boston by 1685. Clan Morrison.

MORTIMER. A territorial surname of Norman-French origin found in Scotland since the twelfth century. Alexander Mortimer, a Jacobite, was exiled to Maryland in 1716.

MORTON. A surname of territorial origin taken from both Morton in Dumfries-shire, and Myrton (later Morton) in east Fife. The placenames both mean *'moor'* or *'myre-town'*. A surname found in Scotland since the thirteenth century. Robert Morton emigrated to Jamaica in 1731, and Patrick Morton, a Royalist prisoner of war, was transported to New England in 1652.

MOSSMAN. A Dutch or Flemish occupational surname, meaning *'gardener'*, introduced into Scotland by the fifteenth century. James Mossman, a Covenanter, was transported to the West Indies in 1678, while George Mossman was in Charleston in the 1680s.

MOULTRIE, MOUTRAY. A surname recorded in Scotland since the twelfth century. John Moultrie settled in Charleston in 1729

MOUNCEY. A Norman-French surname introduced into Scotland by the thirteenth century. Margaret Mongey (!) arrived in Pennsylvania in 1697.

MOUNT. Possibly a descriptive surname indicating a placed of residence, probably from the Gaelic word *'monadh'* meaning 'hill'. Examples date from the twelfth century. William Mount settled in East New Jersey in 1685, and George Mount was banished to the American Plantations in 1674.

MOWAT, MOAT, MOUATT. A territorial surname of Norman French origin introduced into Scotland in the twelfth century. John Mowatt, from Edinburgh, was transported to Barbados in 1663, and a group of Mowats settled in Georgia in 1774. Some Mowats claim allegiance to the Clan Sutherland.

MOWBRAY, MOUBRAY. Derived from the barony of Mombray in Normandy. This territorial surname was found in Scotland by the twelfth century. Arthur Mowbray was a surgeon in South Carolina before 1746.

MOYES. A patronymic based on the French equivalent of 'Moses'. Possibly introduced from Flanders in the thirteenth century. James and William Moyes, both coopers from Fife, sailed for Darien in 1698.

MUDIE, MOODY. Possibly from the Anglo-Saxon word *'modig'* meaning 'brave', used as a surname in Scotland since the thirteenth century. More common in Angus and in Orkney. Ingram Moodie died in Massachusetts during 1693, David Mudie, from Montrose, settled in East New Jersey in 1684, while James Mudie was a cooper at Hudson Bay around 1683.

MUIRHEAD. A descriptive surname indicating residence *'at the head of the moor'*. Taken from one of a number of places bearing that name, and used as a surname since around 1400. Dr Ebenezer Muirhead, from Dumfries-shire, settled in Providence, Rhode Island, by 1754, and John Muirhead was a merchant in Philadelphia by 1699.

THE SCOTTISH SURNAMES OF COLONIAL AMERICA

MULLIGAN. A surname from County Donegal. Hugh and John Mulligan were admitted to the Scots Charitable Society of Boston in 1684 and 1685 respectively.

MUNCKLAND, MONKLAND. A territorial surname derived from Monkland in Lanarkshire, indicating land owned by an order of monks. A surname since around 1300. Roger Munckland died in Darien in 1698.

MUNDILL. A Norman French surname originally *'De Mandeville'*. Found in Scotland by the late thirteenth century particularly in the south west. John Mundill, a Covenanter, was transported to East New Jersey in 1685, and John Mondell, a Jacobite, was transported to Virginia in 1716.

MUNGALL. Based on a place in Falkirk, probably of Gaelic origin bearing the prefix *'moine'* meaning 'moor'. Dating from the thirteenth century as a surname. 'William Munckbell'(?), a Royalist prisoner of war, was transported to New England in 1652.

MURCHIE. An abbreviated form of MacMurchie in use since the sixteenth century. William Murchie, a weaver from Paisley, emigrated to New York in 1774. Clan Mackenzie.

MURCHISON. An Anglicisation of McMurchie (see above), used since the fifteenth century. Duncan and John Murchison, settled on the Kingsborough Patent, New York, in 1773, and relocated to Ontario in 1783.

MURDOCH. A Gaelic surname with origins dating back to the medieval period. David Murdoch died in New York in 1687, and John Murdoch was in Boston by 1691. Clan McPherson.

MURISON. A patronymic which is largely localised in north east Scotland. Examples date back to the fifteenth century. Reverend George Murison, from Aberdeen, died in Connecticut during 1708.

MURRAY. A territorial surname derived from Moray and adopted as a surname by a Fleming named Freskin around 1200. A surname normally associated with Perthshire. Alexander Murray, a schoolmaster from Aberdeenshire, settled in Pennsylvania in 1762, and David Murray, from Orkney, settled in Georgia in 1775. Clan Murray.

MURROW. An abbreviation of McMuireadhaigh (see MacMurray above). Found in Scotland and in Ulster. James and John Murrow, prisoners of war, were transported to New England in 1651

MUSCHET, MUSHET. A territorial surname derived from Montfiquet in Normandy and introduced into Scotland by the mid-twelfth century. David Mushet, a farmer from Stirling, emigrated to New York in 1775, and Robert Mushet, a merchant from Dunbarton, settled in Jamaica by 1774.

MYLES. Perhaps from the Latin word *'miles'* meaning 'soldier' or 'knight', or possibly from a Gaelic word *'mael'* meaning 'bald'. A surname recorded in Scotland since the seventeenth century. George Miles, a Jacobite, was transported to the American colonies in 1748.

NAIRN. Derived from the burgh of the same name and used as a surname since the fourteenth century. Reverend William Nairn was sent to Bermuda in 1722, and James Nairn, a smith from Paisley, emigrated to New York in 1774.

NAISMITH. An occupational surname derived from the trade of *'knife-smith'*. A surname found in Scotland since the fifteenth century. John Nasmith, a merchant from Edinburgh, died in Virginia in 1747, while John Naismith, a Jacobite from Dundee, was transported to Maryland in 1747.

NAPIER. An occupational surname originating with the task of being responsible for napery, such as table-linen. A surname recorded in Scotland since the thirteenth century. William Napier, a surgeon from Glasgow, died in Charleston by 1735, and Patrick Napier died in Virginia during 1669.

NEIL, NEAL. An abbreviation of MacNeil, (see above), and in use as a surname since the fifteenth century. Andrew Neill was in Boston by 1659, and Michael Neal, a Jacobite, was transported to the American colonies in 1747. Clan MacNeil.

NEILSON. A patronymic meaning 'son of Neil' used since the fourteenth century. James Neilson was transported to Virginia in 1696 and George Neilson, a Jacobite, was exiled to Maryland in 1716. Some Neilsons are connected with Clan Mackay and others with Clan MacNeil.

NEVERY. Possibly a variation of Niddry via Nithry. Originally a placename in West Lothian meaning 'new settlement'. James Nevery, a Jacobite, was exiled to Maryland in 1716.

NEWBIGGING. Descriptive indicating a place of residence, from the term meaning *' a new[farm] building'*. There are several such place

names in Scotland. Andrew Newbigging was transported to the
American Plantations in 1679.

NEWLANDS. A territorial surname derived either from a site in
Kincardineshire or another in Peebles-shire. It dates as a surname
since the fifteenth century.

NEWTON. A descriptive term indicating a place of residence – the *'new
town'*. There are many such place-names and usually are found
within a parish in close proximity to an existing settlement. Used as
a surname since the thirteenth century. John Newton, a schoolmaster
from Haddington, was transported to the American colonies in 1762.

NICHOLL, NICOLL, NICOL. A diminutive of Nicholas recorded in
Scotland since the sixteenth century. Barbara Nicol from Aberdeen
was transported to the American colonies in 1728, and Dr John
Nicoll from Edinburgh settled in New York before 1712.

NICHOLSON, NICOLSON. A patronymic, meaning 'son of Nichol',
recorded since the fifteenth century. John Nicolson was transported
to East New Jersey in 1684, and John Nicholson, a Jacobite, was
transported to South Carolina in 1716.

NIMMO. A variation of Nemoch a surname recorded in the fifteenth
century James Nimmo, a Jacobite, was exiled to Antigua in 1716.

NINIAN. A medieval Scots saint's name which was adopted as a
Christian name and later, by the sixteenth century, as a surname.
Grizel Ninian was banished to Virginia in 1772.

NISBET, NESBIT. A territorial surname originating in the barony of
Nesbit in Berwickshire. The meaning of the name is not clear but
may include the Old Norse prefix *'noes'* meaning 'promontary' or
'projecting land'. Examples of this surname date back to the
twelfth century. and later in Ireland John Nisbet, a Covenanter from
Glasgow, was transported to Carolina in 1684, Mungo Nisbet was
in Boston by 1695, and Thomas Nesbit from Belfast settled in
Pennsylvania in 1753.

NIVEN, NEVIN. Originally a Gaelic name *'Naomhin'* meaning 'little
saint'. Most early examples come from south-west Scotland and date
from the thirteenth century. William Niven, a Covenanter and
farmer, was transported to East New Jersey in 1685, and another
William Niven was transported to the American colonies in 1775.

NOBLE. A surname introduced by Anglo-Norman immigrants in the
twelfth century. Most of the very early examples come from south-

east Scotland. William Noble, a Jacobite, was exiled to Virginia in 1716, and another William Noble was in Boston by 1757.

NORN. An Orcadian surname of Norse origin with examples dating from the seventeenth century. John Norn, from Orkney, settled in Georgia in 1775.

NORRIE. An unusual surname with an unknown origin, which has been recorded in Scotland since around 1400. Robert Norie, from Dalkeith, perished on the Darien Expedition of 1698.

NORVILLE. A Norman-French surname introduced into Scotland by the fourteenth century. Adam Norvil, a Jacobite, was transported to Maryland in 1747.

NUTTER. Possibly a variant of *'Notare'* recorded in Oxford during 1275. James Nutter, from Roxburghshire, was transported to the American colonies in 1771.

OCHILTREE. A territorial surname taken from lands in Linlithgow. Examples date from the late fourteenth century. Daniel and Hugh Ochiltree were transported to Virginia in 1696.

OCHTERLONIE, AUCHTERLONIE. Territorial, taken from a Gaelic placename in Angus. It bears the prefix *'uachdar'* meaning 'upland'. It has been used as a surname since the thirteenth century. Patrick Ouchterlony died in Maryland during 1753, and David Ochterlony was a mariner in Boston before 1767.

OGILVY, OGILVIE, OGILBIE. Territorial, derived from a barony in Angus, and used as a surname since the thirteenth century. Patrick Ogilvy was in Boston by 1712, William Ogilvie died in Virginia during 1750, and James Ogilvy, a merchant, died in Charleston in 1745.

OGSTON. Territorial, possibly from 'Hogeston' in Moray, or from 'Hogyston' in Angus. The surname has been recorded since the thirteenth century. It means *'the settlement of Hogg'*. James Ogston, a Jacobite, was exiled to Virginia in 1716.

OLIPHANT. A Norman surname introduced into Scotland in the twelfth century though originally it appears as 'Olifard'. Dr David Oliphant settled in Charleston before 1772, and William Oliphant was banished to East New Jersey in 1685.

OLIVER. An occupational surname based on the French word *'olivier'* meaning an 'olive picker or merchant'. Found in Scotland since the twelfth century. James Oliver, a Covenanter from Edinburgh, was transported to Jamaica in 1685, and Thomas Oliver, a blacksmith, emigrated to Georgia in 1775.

OMAN, OMAND. A surname of Norse origin found in the Northern Isles from the sixteenth century onwards. Mary and Daniel Oman emigrated to Philadelphia in 1775, and Henry Omand was in Boston by 1766.

ORAM, OREM, ORM. A surname which may originate from two distinct sources. It may come for the Norse word for a 'serpent' or it may be a contaction of an English placename bearing the suffic *'ham'* meaning village. As a surname it can be traced back to around 1300. Archibald Oram arrived in Virginia in 1666, and James Orem was bound for New England in 1721.

ORMISTON. A territorial surname meaning *'the settlement of Orm'*. There are three places named Ormiston in Scotland, one in East Lothian, another in Roxburghshire and also near Perth. 'Orm' is derived from a Norse word meaning 'worm' or 'serpent'. The surname dates from the early twelfth century. Thomas Ormiston, a merchant from Edinburgh, settled in Savannah in 1736, and Joseph Ormiston was in East New Jersey by 1699.

ORR. A surname of unknown origin though possibly from the Gaelic word *'odhar'* meaning 'gray'. Examples date from the thirteenth century. A common surname in Renfrewshire and Glasgow. James Orr was in York County, New England, by 1675, and Robert Orr arrived in Maryland during 1674.

ORROCK. A territorial surname based on lands of that name in Fife. Used as a surname since the thirteenth century. Alexander Orrock, a Jacobite, was transported to Maryland in 1716.

OSBURNE. A patronymical surname originating in the Norse personal name *'Asbjorn'* meaning 'divine bear'. A personal name in the medieval period which gradually became adopted as a surname. George Osburne left Londonderry for Philadelphia in 1785.

OSWALD. An old Anglo-Saxon personal name which has become adopted as a surname. Andrew Oswald, from Edinburgh, emigrated to Virginia in 1684.

PAGAN. Originally introduced into Scotland as a forename by the Normans it eventually became a surname found in the south west from the sixteenth century. Robert Pagan was a merchant in Maine by 1748, and Alexander Piggan(?) was in New London by 1695.

PAIP, PAPE, POPE. A surname found in northern Scotland since the fourteenth century. James Paip, from Aberdeenshire, was sentenced to banishment to the American colonies in 1775.

PAISLEY. A surname derived from the burgh of Paisley and recorded since the twelfth century. James and John Paisly, from Dumfriesshire, emigrated to Charleston in 1774.

PALMER. This surname originally identified someone who had gone on a pilgrimage to the Holy Land. Examples in Scotland date from around 1200. John Palmer was transported to the American colonies in 1726.

PALSON. A patronymic meaning 'son of Paul'. A surname more common in northern Scotland. Thomas Palson was in Boston by 1657, and Hugh Polson, from Sutherland, settled in Jamaica by 1774. Clan Mackay.

PANTON. Possibly a territorial name as it bears the suffix 'ton', but a place as yet unidentified. A surname used since the thirteenth century. Reverend George Panton settled in Trenton, New Jersey, in 1772, and David Panton, a tailor, was bound for Philadelphia in 1775.

PARK. A territorial surname taken from the lands of Park in Renfrewshire, and used as a surname since the thirteenth century. Isobel Park was transported to Barbados in 1663, and Jean Park settled in Charleston in 1699.

PARKER. Based on the occupation of 'park-keeper'. A surname recorded since the thirteenth century. William Parker was transported to Boston in 1751, and James Parker, a merchant from Glasgow, settled in Jamaica by 1754.

PATERSON. A patronymic meaning 'Patrick's son' which dates back to the fifteenth century. William Paterson had been a merchant in the West Indies before being the promoter of the Bank of England in 1694 and the Darien Company in 1698.

PATON, PATTON. A diminutive of 'Patrick' which has been used as a surname since the sixteenth century, though some result from an Anglicisation of *'MacFadyen'*. Also found in Ulster. Robert Paton, a Covenanter, was transported to Virginia in 1669, and John Paton, a Jacobite, to Maryland in 1747. Some claim allegiance to Clan McLaren and others to MacLaine of Lochbuie.

PATTULLO. A surname of territorial origin derived from the land of Pittilloch, a placename which bears the Pictish prefix *'Pit'* meaning 'a share of land' and the Gaelic word *'tulach'* meaning 'hillock'. There are two such places, one in Fife and the other in Perthshire. A surname recorded since the late thirteenth century. James and John Pattullo, Jacobites, were transported to Virginia in 1716.

PAUL. A patronymic in use since at least the sixteenth century. Reverend James Paull settled in Bermuda in 1720, and John Paul, a farmer from Glasgow, emigrated to New York in 1774.

PEACOCK. A surname recorded in Scotland since the thirteenth century. James Peacock, from Ayrshire, was banished to America in 1753, and Robert Peacock was in Boston by 1724.

PEADY, PEDDIE. Diminutives of Peter. Recorded in Angus and Perthshire since the fifteenth century. John Peady was in Boston by 1699, and William Peddie immigrated into East New Jersey in 1685.

PEARSON, PIERSON. A patronymic signifying the 'son of Pierre or Peter' which has been used in Scotland since the thirteenth century. John Pearson arrived in Maryland in 1674, and Elspeth Pearson, a rioter, was transported to the American colonies in 1773.

PEDAN, PEDDIN. An diminutive of 'Patrick' used in west central Scotland as a forename and since the seventeenth century as a surname. Alexander Peddin was transported to the West Indies in 1678.

PEEBLES. A territorial surname derived from either the burgh of that name or from lands near Arbroath of the same title. David Peebles settled at Powell's Creek, Virginia, in 1647, and Alexander Peebles, sailed from Ayr to the West Indies in 1681.

PENMAN. Based on *'Penmaen'* an old British placename, meaning 'head of the rock' in the eastern Borders, and used as a surname since the sixteenth century. Edward Penman, an Edinburgh merchant, settled in Charleston by 1784.

PERKLE. A very rare surname of unknown origin. James Perkle, a printer from Edinburgh, emigrated to Maryland in 1774.

PETER. A patronymic found in north east Scotland since the sixteenth century. John Peter, a Jacobite, was transported to Virginia in 1716, and Thomas Peters, a Glasgow merchant, was bound for Boston in 1685.

PETRIE. A diminutive of Peter and of Patrick used as a surname since the sixteenth century. James Petrie, a Jacobite transportee, landed on Martinique in 1747, and Peter Petrie, from Orkney, settled in Georgia in 1774.

PETTY. Probably from two origins, (1) from the French word *'petite'* meaning 'small', or from (2) a place near Inverness of that name. Used as a surname since the thirteenth century. John Petty, a Covenanter, was banished to the American Plantations in 1685

PHILLIP, PHILP. A patronymic used in Scotland since the thirteenth century. Margaret Philip, from Edinburgh, emigrated to Philadelphia in 1775, and John Philp was the Governor of St Martins, Dutch West Indies, in 1728.

PICKEN. A surname of French origin found mainly in Ayrshire since the seventeenth century. William Picken, a farmer from Argyll, settled in North Carolina in 1774.

PIGGOTT. A surname of French origin, possibly originally *'Picot'*, found in Scotland since the fourteenth century. Alexander Piggott, a Jacobite from Angus, was deported to Jamaica in 1747.

PIRRIE, PIRIE, PERRY. Possibly a diminutive of *'Pierre'* the French form of 'Peter'. A surname dating back to the sixteenth century and found mainly in the north-east and around Glasgow. Margaret Pirie, from Banff, was transported to Virginia in 1749, and Joseph Pirie, from Ayrshire, was transported to the American colonies in 1775.

PITCAIRN. Territorial, derived from the lands of Pitcairn in Fife and used as a surname since the thirteenth century. The name is unusual in that it bears the Pictish prefix *'Pit'* meaning 'a share of land', plus *'cairn'* Gaelic for 'a pile of stones'. Major Robert Pitcairn died at Bunker Hill, and another Robert Pitcairn was an innkeeper in Jamaica around 1780.

PITSCOTTIE. Another name of territorial origin, also from Fife. The few early examples of the surname come from Perth. The name is partly Pictish and partly Gaelic, the latter section comes from the word *'sgotan'* and the name has been translated as 'the croft with the little flock'. A very rare surname. Colin Pitscottie took part in the Darien Expedition of 1699.

PITTENDREICH. This surname comes in a number of variations and is derived from a number of places in eastern Scotland. Another name which bears the Pictish prefix *'Pit'* followed by a Gaelic term.

Robert Pettenreck, an accountant, emigrated to Jamaica in 1684, and William Pendrich arrived in Georgia in 1734.

PITTERKIN, PETERKIN. A diminutive of 'Peter' meaning 'little Peter'. A surname recorded in Scotland since the fifteenth century. Thomas Pitterkin emigrated to Philadelphia in 1775

PITTIGREW, PETTIGREW. A surname associated with Lanarkshire since the thirteenth century. William Pettigrew was a physician in Boston in 1766, and James Pittigrew emigrated to Charleston in 1774.

POLLOCK. A descriptive surname indicating a place of residence. The name is said to be British meaning *'little pool'* a place located near Glasgow, and used as a surname since the twelfth century. Reverend William Pollock settled on James Island, South Carolina, before 1706, and John Pollock, a Covenanter, was transported to East New Jersey in 1685.

POLSON. (see Palson, above). Hugh Polson, from Sutherland, settled in Jamaica before 1774.

POLWART. Territorial, derived from Polworth in Berwickshire, and used as a surname since around 1200 AD. John Polwart emigrated to Georgia in 1734.

PORTEOUS. A surname found in south east Scotland since the fifteenth century. Possibly a contraction of 'port-house' the entrance to a castle, indicating a place of residence. Robert Porteous was a founder member of the Scots Charitable Society of Boston in 1657.

PORTER. An occupational surname, from the French *'portier'* or 'doorkeeper', recorded in Scotland since the thirteenth century, also in Ulster since the Plantation.. Francis Porter was transported to America in 1755.

PORTERFIELD. Territorial, derived from the lands of Porterfield in Renfrewshire. Porterfield was the name given to ground given to the porter of Paisley Abbey in the medieval period. William Porterfield settled in Pensacola, West Florida, before 1767.

POTT. Probably a surname of English origin which has been recorded in Scotland since the sixteenth century. Anthony Pott, from Jedburgh, was transported to Barbados in 1666, and Thomas Potts, a Jacobite, was banished to Maryland in 1716.

THE SCOTTISH SURNAMES OF COLONIAL AMERICA

POUSTIE. Possibly a diminutive of the French surname *'Poste'* meaning 'pillory'. John Poustie, a Jacobite from Edinburgh, was transported to the American colonies in 1748.

POUSTOUN. Territorial, meaning *'the town or settlement of Pow'*. John Poustoun settled in Maryland by 1634.

POWRIE. Territorial, a surname taken from the lands of Powrie near Dundee, and recorded since the fourteenth century. William Powrie, from Peebles-shire, died in Barbados in 1648, and John Powrie landed in Georgia in1734.

PRATT. A surname, possibly of English origin, recorded in Scotland since the twelfth century. Thomas Pratt was bound for Darien in 1698, and John Pratt was in Boston by 1694.

PRESSOCH, PRESSAU. A territorial surname from Glen Esk in Angus. Examples of the surname and variants date from the seventeenth century. David Preshaw was in Boston by 1712.

PRIDE, PRYDE. A surname of unknown origin found in Scotland since the thirteenth century, many of the early examples being recorded in Fife. David Pride, a shoemaker from Fife, emigrated to Philadelphia in 1775.

PRIMROSE. Territorial, derived from lands of that name near Dunfermline. In use as a surname since the fourteenth century. Nicol Primrose, a merchant from Musselburgh, settled in Charleston in 1780

PRINGLE. Territorial, originally 'Hopringle', possibly from *'Hop prjonn gil'*, Norse, meaning 'the narrow valley of Prjonn', a location in Roxburghshire. A surname since the fourteenth century. Dr Robert Pringle died in Philadelphia in 1775, and Walter Pringle the Governor of Dominica died in 1768.

PROCTOR. An occupational surname based on the French word *'procuratour'* meaning 'an attorney' or 'an agent'. Recorded in Scotland since the fifteenth century. Joseph Proctor, a Jacobite, was transported to Antigua in 1716, and William Proctor, from Banff, died in Amelia County, Virginia, in 1761.

PROPHET. A surname of unknown origin which has been recorded in north-east Scotland since the thirteenth century. Sylvester Prophet, a Jacobite, was transported to Virginia in 1716

PROUDFOOT. A descriptive surname of English origin found in Scotland since the thirteenth century. Reverend James Proudfoot went to America in 1754, and John Proudfoot, an Edinburgh hairdresser, emigrated to Virginia in 1774.

PROVAN. Territorial, based on a district in Glasgow, probably derived from *'prebenda'* lands once owned by Glasgow Cathedral. Examples of the surname date from around 1200. Matthew Provan settled in Maryland by 1726, and Robert Provan, a shopbreaker, was transported to Virginia in 1775.

PROVOST. Occupational, from the office of provost or chief magistrate of a burgh. John Provest emigrated fron Stornaway to Philadelphia in 1775.

PULLAR. Probably descriptive indicating 'a dweller by a pool'. Charles Pullar emigrated to Baltimore in 1775.

PURDIE. Probably derived from the Anglo-Saxon name *'Purda'*, examples date from the thirteenth century. Hugh Purdie, from Glasgow, was in Boston by 1750.

RAE, RAY. A surname found throughout Scotland since the thirteenth century. Sometimes Rae is a diminutive of *'MacRae'*. John Rae settled in Georgia during 1738, Reverend John Rae died in Williamsburg, South Carolina, in 1761, and Francis Ray landed in New York in 1741.

RAESIDE. An unidentified placename. Robert Raeside landed in Boston in 1766

RAIN. Possibly from the Gaelic *'rath chain'* meaning 'fort of the tribute', a surname found in south west Scotland since the twelfth century. John Rain emigrated from Kirkcudbright to New York in 1774.

RAITT, RAITH. This surname is based on the Gaelic word *'rath'* meaning a 'fort' and originated in a number of sites in Scotland, in particular Perthshire, Nairn and Fife. John Rait, from Montrose, died in Nevis during 1675, Margaret Raitt, from Montrose, died in Virginia during 1714, and Alexander Rait, from Bervie, was in Boston by 1746.

RALSTON. A territorial surname based on lands of that name in Ayrshire. The name possibly signifies the *'town of Ralph'*, and dates from the thirteenth century. Alexander Ralston settled in New Hampshire in 1773, William Ralston was in Boston by 1698, and David Ralston, a merchant from Glasgow, settled in Virginia by 1762.

RAMAGE. Possibly from the French word for 'wild', recorded in Scotland since around 1300 AD. Alexander Ramage, from Linlithgow, was in Boston by 1765.

RAMSAY. The surname, which means *'ram's island'*, is territorial and originated in the English Midlands, was brought to Scotland by the Anglo-Normans in the twelfth century. Reverend Gilbert Ramsay settled in Barbados by 1689, Margaret Ramsay was transported to Barbados in 1663, and John Ramsay, a Jacobite, was exiled to Virginia in 1716.

RANALD, RONALD. A patronymic derived from the Gaelic personal name *'Raonull'* which comes from the Norse *'Rognvaldr'* meaning 'ruler from the gods'. Recorded as a surname since the fifteenth century. Reverend Alexander Ronald settled in Virginia in 1760, Francis Ranald, a Jacobite, was transported to Barbados in 1747, and William Ronald emigrated to East New Jersey in 1684.

RANALDSON, RONALDSON. Alias 'son of Ronald' (see above). Examples date from the fifteenth century. James Rannoldson, a Jacobite, was transported to Jamaica in 1747.

RANDAL. Derived from the Norse personal name *'Rondulfr'* or 'shield wolf' and used as a surname since the fifteenth century. Robert Randal, a printer from Edinburgh, emigrated to Maryland in 1774.

RANKEN, RANKIN. A diminutive of Ranald(?), 'Ran' plus the suffix 'kin' meaning 'little'. A surname traditionally localised in Glasgow and Ayrshire since the fifteenth century. Hugh Rankin, a barber from saltcoats, settled in Philadelphia in 1774, John Ranken, a Jacobite, was transported to Charleston in 1716, and Hugh Rankine emigrated to Jamaica in 1773.

RATTRAY. A territorial surname originating either in the name of a barony in Perthshire, or a site in Aberdeenshire, and used as a surname since the thirteenth century. The name probably includes the prefix *'rath'* meaning 'fort'. Ann Rattray, from Aberdeen, was banished to Maryland in 1728, James Rattray, from Angus, emigrated to Antigua in 1728, and John Rattray, a judge, died in Charleston during 1761.

REACH, REOCH, RIACH. A descriptive surname taken from the Gaelic adjective *'riabhach'* meaning 'greyish'. Used as a surname since the fifteenth century. Henry Rich was in Boston by 1731, and Janet Reach, from Orkney, settled in Georgia in 1775.

REDFORD. A descriptive name used to indicate a place of residence – 'by the red ford'. Examples of the surname date from the sixteenth century. Thomas Redford emigrated to East New Jersey in 1684, and Samuel Redford died in Freehold, New Jersey, by 1711.

REDLAND. Territorial, derived from Redland in Orkney. Examples of the surname date from the seventeenth century. Magnus Redland, from Orkney, died in Maine during 1772.

REDPATH. Territorial, based on a place name in Berwickshire, and used as a surname since the thirteenth century. John Ridpath, from Edinburgh, was banished to the American Plantations in 1662

REID. Descriptive, the old form of the word 'red', indicating that the person so-named had a ruddy complexion or red hair. Used as a surname since the medieval period. Alexander Reid, a Jacobite, was transported to Maryland in 1716 and died there in 1718, John Reid, a gardener, settled in East New Jersey in 1683, and William Reid settled in Virginia by 1775. Some Reids are affiliated to the Clan Donnachaidh alias Robertson.

REIDIE. Territorial, originating in Reedie near Kirriemuir, Angus, and used as a surname since the sixteenth century. David Reidie settled at Port Nelson, Hudson Bay, in 1683.

REIRIE. Possibly a version of the Gaelic name *'MacRyrie'*. David Reirie, a Jacobite from Caithness, was transported to the colonies in 1748.

REITH. (see Raitt above). Ann Reith, from Fife, was banished to the American colonies in 1774.

RENFREW. Territorial, derived from the burgh of Renfrew and used as a surname since the thirteenth century. Possibly a British name *'rhen friu'* meaning 'flowing brook'. Janet Renfrew, from Paisley, emigrated to New York in 1774.

RENNIE, RANNIE. Diminutives of 'Reynold' or 'Ranold' (see above), which have been used as surnames since the fourteenth century. John and Marion Rennie, Covenanters, were banished to East New Jersey in 1685, William Rannie was transported to America in 1767, and Reverend Robert Renney settled in Overwharton, Virginia, in 1764.

RENTON. Territorial, an Anglo-Saxon place name in Berwickshire meaning the *'settlement of Ren'*, possibly an abbreviation of *'Raegen'*. A surname used since the twelfth century. James Renton, a Jacobite, was transported to Maryland in 1716, and Alexander Renton, a surveyor, settled in Boston by 1729.

RENWICK. Territorial, derived from the lands of Renwick in Cumberland. Examples of the surname in Scotland date from the seventeenth century. John Renwick, a Covenanter from Wigtown, was banished to the American Plantations in 1684.

RESTON. An Anglo-Saxon place name in Berwickshire meaning the *'village of Ris'*, which has been used as a surname since the twelfth century. James Reston, a Covenanter, was transported to East New Jersey in 1685.

REYNOLD. (see Ranald above). David Reynolds was in Boston by 1685, and Alexander Reynolds was in Georgia by 1740.

REYNOLDSON. (see Ranaldson above) James Reynoldson, a Jacobite from Fettercairn, was transported to the American colonies in 1747.

RHEA. (see Ray above). Robert Rhea settled in East New Jersey in 1685.

RHIND, RYND. Territorial, taken from the name of a parish in Perthshire, a gaelic name *'roinn'* meaning 'a point of land'. Used as a surname since the fourteenth century. William Rhind emigrated to Pennsylvania in 1731, and David Rhind, a schoolmaster, settled in Charleston by 1765.

RICHARD. An Anglo-Saxon personal name meaning *'powerfully rich'* used as a surname since the sixteenth century. Thomas Richard, a Covenanter from Ayrshire, was transported to Jamaica in 1685, and John Richards settled in Boston by 1720.

RICHARDSON. A patronymic meaning 'son of Richard' used as a surname since the fourteenth century. Bessie Richardson was bound for East New Jersey in 1685, and William Richardson, an Edinburgh printer, emigrated to Maryland in 1774.

RICHMOND. Territorial, derived from Richmond in England, and used as a surname in Scotland since the seventeenth century. Helen Richmond, from Edinburgh, was transported to Virginia in 1696, and James Richmond, a cattle thief from Glasgow, was transported to the American colonies in 1772.

RIDDELL. This surname may be of two origins, it may have been a French surname introduced by the Anglo-Normans during the twelfth century, or it may derive from Rydale in Yorkshire. Reverend Archibald Riddell settled in Woodbridge, East New

Jersey, in 1685, Dr George Riddell died in Virginia during 1779, and Hugh Riddell, a Covenanter, was banished to New York in 1683.

RIDDOCH, RADDOCK. A surname, probably of Gaelic origin, recorded since the sixteenth century. Dr Colin Riddoch settled in Virginia by 1768, John Riddock emigrated to New York in 1775, and Samuel Raddock died in Annapolis in 1769.

RIGG. Probably from the Scandinavian word *'ryg'* meaning 'ridge'. A surname since the sixteenth century. William Rig emigrated to East New Jersey in 1685, and Alexander Rigg died in Charleston by 1771.

RITCHIE. An abbreviation of Richard, used as a surname since the fourteenth century. John Ritchie was transported to Maryland in 1771, and William Ritchie, a Jacobite, was transported to Jamaica in 1747.

ROBB. A diminutive of Robert, used as a surname since the sixteenth century. Elizabeth Robb, a Jacobite transportee, landed on Martinique in 1747, and Hugh Robb, a Glasgow tailor, emigrated to New York in 1774.

ROBERTON. A name of territorial origin, derived from Roberton in Lanarkshire, a village established by a medieval Flemish settler called Robert. Used as a surname since the thirteenth century. John Roberton was in Boston by 1713.

ROBERTSON. One of the most common Scottish patronymics, meaning *'son of Robert'*, recorded since the fourteenth century. Reverend George Robertson settled in Dinwiddie County, Virginia, by 1693, Leonard Robertson, a Jacobite, was banished to Maryland in 1716, and Patrick Robertson was a merchant in New London, Connecticut, by 1772. Clan Robertson or Donnachaidh.

ROBINSON. Meaning 'son of Robin' a diminutive of 'Robert', used as a surname since the fifteenth century. James Robinson, a Glasgow merchant, settled in Falmouth, Virginia, by 1767, and John Robinson, a Jacobite, was transported to St Kitts in 1716.

ROBISON, ROBESON, ROBSON. Alias 'son of Rob' a diminutive of 'Robert', a surname recorded, especially on the Borders, since the fifteenth century. John Robison was banished to the West Indies in 1728, and Robert Robson sailed from Newcastle bound for Georgia in 1775.

ROCHHEAD, ROUGHEAD. Presumably a descriptive surname. Examples date from the thirteenth century. James Rochead, from Edinburgh, was a merchant in New York before 1740.

RODAN. A territorial surname, probably derived from Roddam in northern England. Homer Rodan emigrated to Virginia in 1698.

ROGER, RODGER. A patronymic, used as a surname since the fifteenth century. Reverend John Roger settled in Pennsylvania during 1770, and John Rogers settled in Maryland by 1750

ROGERSON. Otherwise *'son of Roger'* a surname recorded in Scotland since the fifteenth century. Janet Rogerson emigrated from Dumfries to Prince Edward Island in 1775.

ROLL, RULE, ROLLO. From *'Roul'* a Norman-French version of 'Rolf'. John Roll, a gardener from Aberdeen, emigrated to Maryland in 1774.

ROLLAND. A surname introduced by the Anglo-Normans in the twelfth century. Henry Rolland, a carpenter from Culross, settled in Charleston before 1774, and William Roland was in Boston by 1725.

ROME. A surname, possibly derived from a place in Yorkshire, found in Dumfries-shire since the sixteenth century. George Rome, a Covenanter, was transported to Carolina in 1684, and another George Rome was a merchant in Rhode Island before 1776.

ROSE. Possibly an early offshoot of the Clan Ross, the Rose family of Kilravock was established by the fourteenth century. Reverend Charles Rose died in Virginia during 1761, and John Rose died in Jamaica in 1775. Clan Rose.

ROSS. The main family is of Celtic origin and has been located in the district of Ross from which it has taken its name, however there is a Ross family of Ayrshire that migrated north from Yorkshire in the twelfth century and may be of Norman origin. Several Rosses were transported to Boston in 1651. Clan Ross.

ROWAN. This surname may derive from a number of sources: (1) from the Gaelic word *'ruadhan'* for 'red', (2) from a corruption of the surname 'Rolland' (see above), and (3) from the French town of Rouen. The surname appears in Scottish records from the sixteenth century onwards. William Rowan, a cooper, emigrated to Carolina in 1684, and Alexander Rouan emigrated to Jamaica in 1763.

ROWSAY. Territorial, originating in the island of Rowsay in the Orkneys, and used as a surname since the seventeenth century. 'Rowsay' is a corruption of the Norse *'Hrolfsay'* meaning 'Rolf's island'. John Rowsay, a goldsmith from Orkney, settled in Virginia by 1773.

ROXBURGH. Territorial, from the town of that name in the Borders. Originally *'Hroc'sburh'* meaning ' Roc's castle', and used as a surname since the twelfth century. James Roxburgh emigrated to Virginia in 1774, and Robert Roxburgh emigrated to New York in 1775.

ROY. The Gaelic descriptive term *'ruadh'*, meaning 'red', became Anglicised as 'Roy' by the sixteenth century. Donald Roy, a Glasgow tailor, emigrated to New York in 1775, and James Roy, a shipmaster, settled in New York by 1777.

RUDDIMAN. Possibly a variation of the English surname *'Rydeman'* recorded in Huntingdon during the fourteenth century, or *'Rodman'* noted in Ayr around 1500 AD. William Rudiman, from Aberdeen, died in New York during 1769, and Janet Ruddiman, from Montrose, emigrated to New York in 1775.

RUSSELL. A diminutive of 'red' used as a surname since the twelfth century. James Russell, from Edinburgh, was transported to Barbados in 1663, and Reverend Thomas Russell settled in Halifax, Nova Scotia, in 1783.

RUTHERFORD. Territorial, derived from a place name, near Kelso, originally *'hrythera-ford'* an old English term for a 'ford for cattle', and used as a surname by the twelfth century. James Rutherford, a Jacobite, was transported to Maryland in 1716, and John Rutherford of Bowland settled in Wilmington, North Carolina, by 1752.

RUXTON. Possibly an Anglicisation of the Gaelic name *'Reochtan'*. John Ruxton was transported to New England in 1650.

RYMER. An occupational surname indicating a minstrel, a balladeer or a poet. A surname used in Scotland since the thirteenth century. Reverend James Rymer died in Walterborough, South Carolina, in 1755.

SADDLER. An occupational surname dating from the fourteenth century. William Saddler, a merchant, died in St Kitts by 1781

SALMOND. A patronymic based on 'Solomon' and used as a surname since the fifteenth century. George Salmon served in the Virginia Regiment during 1757.

SAMUEL. An uncommon patronymic recorded since the early modern period. George Samuel, a Jacobite transportee, was landed on Martinique in 1747.

SANDELAND. Territorial, derived from the lands of that name in Lanarkshire, and used as a surname since the fifteenth century. James Sandeland was in Boston by 1687, and a James Sandylands, a soldier, was in Delaware in 1668.

SANDEMAN. Possibly a Danish surname, *'Sandemand'*, introduced into early modern Scotland. Examples date from the early seventeenth century and are localised in Perth. Robert Sandeman, from Perth, died in Danbury, Massachusetts, in 1771

SANDERS, SAUNDERS. An abbreviation of *'Alexander'* used as a surname since the fifteenth century. William Saunders, from Angus, emigrated to Philadelphia in 1775.

SANDERSON. A patronymic meaning *'son of Alexander'* which has been used since the fifteenth century. Daniel Sanderson was transported to Virginia in 1668, and Beattie Sanderson was transported to the American Plantations in 1695.

SANDS. A territorial surname derived from lands in west Fife and used as a surname since the fifteenth century. James Sands, a merchant, died in Charleston in 1767, and Alexander Sands emigrated to Philadelphia in 1775.

SANGSTER. An occupational surname denoting a *'singer'* which has been used as a surname since the fifteenth century. Andrew Sangster, a Jacobite, was transported to South Carolina in 1716.

SAVAGE. A Norman-French surname which seems to have reached Scotland via England and Ireland. Edward Savage emigrated to New England in 1727, and Bartholemew Savage, from Dublin, emigrated to Jamaica in 1750.

SCHOLLAR, SCOULLAR. Probably used to indicate a 'scholar' though possibly from the Norse word *'skali'* meaning 'hut'. John Scoullar emigrated to East New Jersey in 1685.

SCOLLAY, SCHOALLA. An Orcadian territorial surname derived from Skail in Sandwick, originally a Norse name *'skali'* meaning a 'shieling'. Robert Schoalla sailed to Darien in 1698, and James Scollay was in Boston by 1713.

SCOTLAND A territorial surname mostly found in west Fife and Clackmannan since the seventeenth century. Lawrence Scotland emigrated to New England in 1699, and John Scotland settled in Antigua by 1773.

SCOTT. A surname recorded in Scotland since the twelfth century, particularly on the Borders and from the seventeenth century in Ulster. John Scott settled in Georgia in 1775, Reverend James Scott was in Stafford County, Virginia, by 1719, and William Scott was a merchant in Charleston before 1765. Clan Scott.

SCOUGAL. A territorial surname derived from lands of that name in East Lothian, and used as a surname since around 1200 AD. Reverend James Scougall settled in Maryland in 1746.

SCROGGIE. A territorial surname taken from a village name in Perthshire and used as a surname since the fifteenth century. John Scroggie settled in Jamaica by 1776.

SCRYMGEOUR. An occupational surname meaning a 'fencing-master', from the Old French word for skirmisher. H. Y. Scrymgeour emigrated to Jamaica in 1774, and James Scrimgeour settled in East New Jersey in 1685.

SEAMAN. A patronymic derived from the Anglo-Saxon personal name *'Seman'*. A rare surname in Scotland though examples date from the thirteenth century. George Seaman, from Leith, died in Charleston during 1769.

SEATON, SETON. Probably a territorial surname meaning *'the settlement of Say'* referring to a village founded by the de Say family in East Lothian, though possibly from *'sea-toun'* indicating a hamlet by the sea. Margaret Seton emigrated to Philadelphia in 1775, James Seaton emigrated to New York in 1774, and R. Seaton, from Cork, emigrated to Philadelphia in 1774.

SELKIRK, SELKRIG. A name of territorial origin based on the burgh of Selkirk and used as a surname since the thirteenth century. Originally *'Selechyrca'* meaning 'church in the hall'. James Selkirk emigrated to New York in 1774, and Robert Selkrig was a merchant in Boston in 1767.

SELLAR, SILLAR, SILVER. An occupational surname, possibly from the middle-English word *'seler'* meaning 'saddler', or from the French word *'celier'* meaning cellar-man. A surname used in Scotland since the thirteenth century. Archibald Silver was in East New Jersey by 1685, and Hugh Sillar, from Argyll, emigrated to North Carolina in 1774.

SEMPLE, SEMPILL, SIMPLE. Possibly corruptions of *'St Paul'*, surnames found in the west of Scotland since the thirteenth century. William Sempill was in Delaware by 1679, and John Semple was a merchant in New York by 1776.

SENIOR, SENZOUR. A descriptive surname recorded in Scotland since the fourteenth century. John and Cicella Senzour emigrated to East New Jersey in 1685, and George Senior was in Georgia by 1760.

SERVICE. Possibly an occupational surname, meaning *'brewer'* or *'tavern-keeper'* from the Norman Franch word *'cervoise'* meaning 'ale'. A surname which has been used in Scotland since the thirteenth century. Samuel Service of Sarviss was in Boston by 1735

SEYMOUR. Probably derived from 'Saint Maur' in northern France. Reverend James Seymour settled in Augusta, Georgia, in 1771.

SHAND. An old Aberdeenshire surname of unknown origin, possibly with the Gaelic prefix *'sean'* meaning 'old'. John Shand, from Aberdeen, died in Boston in 1738, and another John Shand, from Aberdeenshire, emigrated to Jamaica in 1726.

SHANNON, SHANNAN. An Anglicisation of the Gaelic name *'Seanain'* meaning 'old and wise'. Recorded, especially in Dumfries and Galloway, since the sixteenth century. Henry Shannan emigrated to Prince Edward Island in 1775, and Nathaniel Shannon was in Boston by 1691.

SHARP, SHAIRP. A surname, possibly of descriptive origin, used in Scotland since the fifteenth century. Reverend John Sharp emigrated to Virginia in 1699, and Robert Sharp was transported to Jamaica in 1685.

SHAW, SCHAW. This surname is derived from two distinct sources. In the Lowlands the name comes from an Old English word *'scaga'* or an Old Scandinavian word *'skog-r'* or *'skov'* meaning a 'wood'. Whereas the surname in the Highlands is based on an Anglicisation of the Gaelic word *'sithech'*. Examples of the surname date back to the thirteenth century. John Shaw, a cabinetmaker, settled in Annapolis in 1775, and Peter Shaw, a Jacobite, was transported to South Carolina in 1716. Clan Shaw.

SHEARER. An occupational surname describing a 'cloth-cutter'. Examples date back to the fourteenth century. Thomas Shearer settled in East New Jersey in 1685, and Joseph Shirar emigrated to New York in 1774.

SHEDDAN. Possibly a territorial surname from a place near Glasgow. Examples date from the seventeenth century. James Sheddan enlisted in the Pennsylvania Regiment in 1758, and William Ralston Shedden was a merchant in America in 1770.

SHEPHERD. An occupational surname used in Scotland since the thirteenth century. John Shepherd, a Jacobite from Montrose, landed in Maryland in 1747.

SHERIFF. An occupational surname derived from the office of 'shire-reeve', 'reeve' meaning 'steward'. A surname in Scotland since the fourteenth century. John Sheriff settled on the island of St Thomas before 1783, and William Sherriff was the commissary at Annapolis by 1717.

SHIELDS, SHIELS, SHIEL. A descriptive surname based on the Scottish word meaning a *'hut'*, from the Norse word *'skali'*. James Shields was transported to Virginia in 1666, John Shields was a runaway servant in Maryland during 1770, and Martin Shields, from Ireland, emigrated to Maryland in 1774.

SHILESTON. A very rare surname based on an unidentified location. Thomas Shileston, a Covenanter, was transported to East New Jersey in 1685.

SHIRMLAW. A territorial surname of unidentified origin. The suffix *'law'* means 'hill'. William Shirmlaw emigrated to Philadelphia in 1775.

SHIRRAS. A surname, recorded since the fifteenth century, of unknown origin mainly found in Aberdeenshire. Alexander Shirras, a merchant, settled in Charleston about 1781.

SHISH. Possibly a variant of the surname 'Shiach' based on the word *'sitech'* the Gaelic for 'wolf'. James Shish, a Covenanter, was banished to the American Plantations in 1670.

SHORT. A descriptive surname recorded since the medieval period. George Short, a forger, was transported to the American colonies in 1766.

SHUNGERS. A very obscure surname of unknown origin. Alexander Shonger, a Jacobite, was transported to Virginia in 1716, and John Shungers, also a Jacobite, from Angus, was transported to the West Indies in 1747.

SIBBALD. Originally an Anglo-Saxon personal name which has been used as a surname in Scotland since the thirteenth century. David Sibbald was a planter in Jamaica around 1772.

SIBBET. An variation of 'Sibbald' also used since the thirteenth century. Peter Sibbet, from Haddington, died in Virginia before 1678.

SIM, SIME, SYM, SYME. All diminutives of Simon and used as surnames since the fifteenth century. Hugh Sym was in Georgia by 1770, and Alexander Sim arrived in Maryland during 1674.

SIMPSON, SIMSON. A patronymic meaning the *'son of Sim'*, a surname in use since the fifteenth century. James Simpson, from Dumfries-shire, settled in Charleston by 1764, and Reverend David Simpson was banished to East New Jersey in 1685.

SINCLAIR. A Norman-French territorial surname that was introduced into Scotland during the twelfth century. Initially the surname was recorded in the vicinity of Edinburgh but later in Caithness and Orkney. Peggy Sinclair, from Jura, settled in North Carolina in 1767, and Richard Sinclair was a merchant in Charleston before 1733.

SKENE. A territorial surname, derived from the lands of Skene in Aberdeenshire, used as a surname since the late thirteenth century. An Anglicised version of a Gaelic name *'sceathin'* meaning 'bush'. John Skene, from Aberdeen, was a Governor of East New Jersey, and Dr James Skene settled in Charleston before 1766. Clan Skene.

SKINNER. An occupational surname used since the fourteenth century. William Skinner died in Perth Amboy in 1758, and Charles Skinner emigrated to Maryland in 1774.

SLATER. An occupational surname used since the fourteenth century. James Slater emigrated to New York in 1774, and Peter Slater, from Orkney, was in Boston by 1750.

SLOANE. An Anglicisation of the Gaelic name *'Sluaghadain'* alias 'a military leader'. Recorded as a surname since around 1500 AD especially in the south-west, also in Ulster. John Sloan emigrated to New York in 1775, and John Sloane settled in Maryland in 1674.

SLOSS. A contracted from of 'Auchencloss', (see above), via the name 'Aslois' used since the seventeenth century. Robert Sloss, a Covenanter from Ayr, was banished to the American Plantations in 1685.

SMALL. A descriptive surname used in Scotland since the fourteenth century. James Small, a Jacobite, was transported to Maryland in 1716, and Robert Small, a barber from Perth, emigrated to Philadelphia in 1775.

SMART. An Old English personal name dating back to the eleventh century. Recorded as a surname in Scotland since the fourteenth century. Alexander Smart was in Boston by 1690, and David Smart settled in New York by 1775.

SMEALL A variant of Small (see above). Elizabeth Smeall was transported to the American colonies in 1768.

SMELLIE, SMYLLIE. Origin unknown. John Smellie, a merchant from Glasgow, settled in Jamaica by 1729, Thomas Smellie, a weaver, emigrated to New York in 1774, and Matthew Smylie settled in North Carolina in 1739..

SMIBERT. An surname of Anglo-Saxon origin. Dr William Smibert was in Boston by 1765.

SMISON. A variant of 'Smithson'

SMITH. A very common surname of occupational origin, which signifies a 'metal worker'. Examples date back to the mediaeval period. Several Jacobites named Smith were banished to the American colonies in 1716 and in 1747.

SMITHSON. Meaning 'son of the smith' and used as a surname since around 1400. John Smithson was in Boston in 1699.

SMOLLETT. A surname of unknown origin which has been associated with Dunbartonshire since the fifteenth century. Benjamin Smollett, a surgeon, settled in New England during 1687.

SNODGRASS. Territorial, based on a place name in Irvine, Ayrshire, which has been used as a surname since the fourteenth century. John Snodgrass, a factor from Glasgow, settled in Goochland, Virginia, before 1776, and Neil Snodgrass, a merchant from Paisley, died in New York in 1782.

SOMERVILLE. A French territorial surname introduced into Scotland by the Anglo-Normans during the twelfth century, and to Ulster by Scots settlers in the seventeenth century. James Somerville was a Virginia militiaman by 1763.

SOUTAR. An occupational name derived from the Norse *'sutare'* or 'shoemaker' and used as a surname since the fourteenth century. John Soutar, a Jacobite from Aberdeenshire, was transported to

Maryland in 1747, and a group of Soutars from Paisley emigrated to New York in 1774.

SPALDING. A territorial surname introduced from England into Scotland by the thirteenth century. Derived from Spalding in Lincolnshire. Alexander Spalding, a Jacobite, was exiled to Maryland in 1716, and James Spalding, an Edinburgh merchant, settled in East Florida by 1772.

SPARK. Derived from the Anglo-Saxon name *'Sparhauoc'* and used as a surname in Scotland since around 1400 AD. Alexander Spark, a schoolmaster from Kincardineshire, settled in Quebec in 1780, and another Alexander Spark, a merchant, died in Westmoreland County, Virginia in 1767.

SPEED. A surname of unknown origin which has been recorded since the fifteenth century. William Speed, a Jacobite, was transported to Maryland in 1747, and another William Speed was a co-founder of the Scots Charitable Society of Boston in 1657.

SPEIR. An occupational name signifying either a watchman, derived from the French word *'espier'*, or a spearman from the English word *'spere'*. Examples date from the thirteenth century, and later in Ulster. Alexander Speir, a clerk, emigrated to North Carolina in 1774, and Joseph Speirs settled in Barbados by 1676.

SPENCE, SPENS, SPENCER. An occupational surname used to describe a man who dispensed resources such as food in a castle or monastery. Adopted as a surname in the fourteenth century. Helen Spence was transported to Virginia in 1696, and John Spencer was a runaway indentured servant in Maryland in 1777.

SPITTLE, SPITTAL. A corruption of the Gaelic word *'spideal'* meaning 'hospital' or 'hospice', and used as a surname since the fourteenth century. James Spittle, a housebreaker, was transported to the American colonies in 1773.

SPROAT, SPROTT, SPRATT. A surname which is probably of Scandinavian origin and found in Scotland since the thirteenth century. William Sprout, a Covenanter, was banished to East New Jersey in 1685, and three Sproats from Kirkcudbrightshire emigrated to New York in 1774.

SPROULE, SPREULL. A surname of unknown origin first recorded in Scotland during the thirteenth century. Andrew Sproule, a merchant in Norfolk, Virginia, died by 1779.

SQUIRE. Occupational, from the office of squire or a knight's attendant. Examples of the surname date back to the thirteenth century. George Squire emigrated to New York in 1774, and William Squire died in Massachusetts.during 1731.

STALKER. A surname of occupational origin, indicating one who stalks animals such as a deer-stalker. Duncan Buie Stalker, from Argyll, was banished to America for cattle rustling in 1766.

STARK. A descriptive name from the Netherlands meaning *'strong'* which has been found in Scotland since the fourteenth century. Donald Stark, from Caithness, was banished to the American colonies in 1769, and Archibald Stark, from Glasgow, died in New Hampshire in 1758.

STARKEY. A diminutive of Stark (see above).

STARRETT, STIRRAT. A surname taken from a former place name in Ayrshire, Stairaird, and used as a surname since the fifteenth century. Also found in Ulster. William Starrett settled in New England in 1735, and David Stirrat, from Gourock, was in Massachusetts by 1786.

STEDMAN, STEEDMAN. An occupational surname derived from the Old English term *'stead-man'* meaning 'farm manager'. James Stedman settled in Georgia by 1768.

STEEL, STEILL. Territorial, derived from one of a number of places in the Lowlands of Scotland, such as Steill (now Ladykirk) in Berwickshire. Hugh Steel was a shipmaster and captain of a Philadelphia based privateer before 1757.

STELLER. Possibly a variant of the Anglo-Saxon occupational name *'steallare'* meaning 'marshal'. John Steller of Scotter arrived in Pennsylvania in 1697.

STEPHEN, STEVEN. Originally a forename used in honor of St Stephen, but by the fifteenth century it had become a surname. Rev. John Stephen was a clergyman in Tobago and later in Maryland before 1784.

STEPHENSON, STEVENSON. A patronymic meaning 'son of Stephen/Steven'. Used as a surname in Scotland since at least the fourteenth century. Robert Stevenson, a bookbinder from Edinburgh, emigrated to Antigua in 1728, Janet Stevenson, from Edinburgh, emigrated to Philadelphia in 1775, and Nathan Stevenson emigrated from Belfast to Philadelphia in 1773.

STEWART, STUART. An occupational surname, ultimately derived
from the Old English term *'stigeweard'* meaning 'sty-warden', later
'steward' indicating a household supervisor. In Scotland the family
commenced with Walter the Steward around 1150. Several
Jacobites named Stewart were exiled to the American colonies in
1716 and also in 1747. Robert Stewart emigrated from Belfast to
Philadelphia in 1773. Clan Stewart.

STILL. A variant of Steel, a relatively uncommon surname with
examples dating from the fifteenth century. John Alexander Still
settled in Hanover, Virginia, before 1776.

STINSON, STEENSON. Variants of Stevenson. Ann Steenson, from
Fife, emigrated to Philadelphia in 1775, and John Stinson arrived in
Maryland in 1674.

STIRK. A descriptive surname, likening an individual to a 'stirk' or
young bullock. Most early examples originate in Fife and date from
the fourteenth century. Reverend George Stirke settled in Bermuda
during 1623, and Benjamin Stirk settled in Georgia in 1761

STIRLING. Territorial, taken from the name of the Royal Burgh. Used
as a surname since the twelfth century. George Stirling died in
Georgia by 1749, and Mabel Stirling was transported to Virginia in
1715.

STITT. A surname of unknown origin. Edward Stitt, a Covenanter, was
transported to Jamaica in 1678.

STOBO, STOBIE. Territorial, taken from a placename in Peebles-shire.
Examples of the surname date back to the twelfth century. Rev.
Archibald Stobo settled in Charleston in 1699, and Adam Stobie was
transported to the West Indies in 1678.

STODDART, STODDARD, STOTHART. An occupational surname
based on the task of *'stot-herd'* a man who supervised bullocks. A
surname found in Scotland since the fourteenth century. Lawrence
Stoddart emigrated to Philadelphia in 1774, and James Stoddart was
in Maryland by 1650.

STORIE. Possibly a descriptive surname based on the Scandinavian word
'stori', meaning 'large', recorded since the thirteenth century.
James Storie was transported to Carolina in 1684.

STORMONTH. Territorial, taken from a district in Perthshire. Based on
a Gaelic name *'starr monadh'* meaning 'twisted hill'. Examples

date from the early sixteenth century. James Stormonth, from Angus, died in St Kitts before 1761.

STRACHAN. Territorial, taken from a place name in Kincardineshire, originally *'Strath Auchin'* from the Gaelic meaning 'valley of the horse'. The surname dates back to around 1200. Adam Strachan, a schoolmaster, was sent to the Leeward Islands in 1700, while John Strachan emigrated to Virginia in 1696.

STRANG. Possibly a descriptive surname equivalent to 'Strong', or from the French *'L'estraunge'* meaning 'foreigner'. Recorded in Scotland as a surname since the thirteenth century. Reverend David Strange was transported to Virginia in 1738, and Christopher Strang, a Covenanter, was banished to East New Jersey in 1685.

STRATTON, STRAITON. Territorial, derived from three or more baronies of that name in Lowland Scotland. Probably based on the Old English meaning *'village on the road'*. In use as a surname since the thirteenth century. James Stretton emigrated to Maryland in 1683, and Thomas Stratton, from Dunnottar, died in Jamaica during 1777.

STROAK, STROCK. Possibly variants of the surname *'Sturrock'* meaning 'sheep farmers' a name localised in Angus. Examples date from the fifteenth century. James Strock, a Jacobite, was transported to Antigua in 1716, and William Stroak, a Jacobite, was transported to Virginia in 1716.

STRONACH. A descriptive surname derived from the Gaelic word *'sronach'* meaning 'nosey'. The surname dates from the fifteenth century with most examples coming from Aberdeenshire. Michael Stronach settled in Georgia in 1738.

STROTHERS, STRUTHERS. An Old English term indicating a 'marsh' or 'swamp'. Recorded as a surname in Scotland since the sixteenth century. A. Strothers was a merchant in Pensacola in 1781, and William Struthers was an Indian trader in Augusta, Georgia, before 1761.

SUMMERS, SYMMER. An occupational surname from the job of 'summoner' found in Scotland since the twelfth century. Alexander and Andrew Symmer, merchants from Edinburgh, settled in Maryland before 1756, while Bartholemew Summers, a butcher from Elgin, emigrated to New York in 1775.

SUTHERLAND. Territorial, taken from the name of the county, originating in the Norse term *'Sudyrland'* meaning 'the southern land'. Used as a surname since the fourteenth century. Several Jacobites named Sutherlands were transported to the West Indies in 1747. Clan Sutherland.

SUTTIE. Possibly based on the territorial name *'de Sudy'* a surname recorded in the early fourteenth century. David Suttie died at Darien in 1698.

SUTTON. Probably originally an English surname. Andrew Sutton, a gentleman emigrated to New York in 1774.

SWAN. Patronymic, originating in the Scandinavian personal name *'Svein'*. Recorded in Scotland since the thirteenth century. John Swan, a Covenanter, was exiled to East New Jersey in 1685, while James Swan went to Hudson Bay in 1684.

SWANSTON. A territorial surname of Anglian origin taken from Swanston, near Edinburgh, meaning *'the tun or settlement of Sven'*. Used as a surname since the thirteenth century. Charles and James Swanston, from Caithness, were transported to the American colonies in 1769.

SWINTON. A territorial surname of Anglian origin taken from Swinton, *'the tun or settlement of Sven'*, in Berwickshire. Used as a surname since the thirteenth century. John Swinton, a Quaker from Roxburghshire, was transported to East New Jersey in 1685, and William Swinton was in Georgia by 1763.

SWORD. A corruption of the Old English personal name *'Siward'*. Examples date from the fourteenth century.Humphrey Sword, a Jacobite, was transported to Virginia in 1716, and John Sword, another Jacobite, was transported to St Kitts, also in 1716.

SYMINGTON. Territorial, taken from Symington in Lanarkshire, originally the village of Simon Lockhart, a medieval knight. A surname in Scotland since the fourteenth century.

TAGGART. An abbreviation of *'MacTaggart'*, see above. John Taggart, a Covenanter, was banished to the American Plantations in 1684

TAILFER, TELFER, A Norman-French occupational surname roughly equivalent to 'blacksmith'. A surname in Scotland since the thirteenth century. Patrick Tailfer, a physician from Edinburgh, settled in Georgia in 1733, and W. Telfair settled in Louisiana by 1764.

TAIS. A variant of the surname Taws, a corruption of the Gaelic name *'Tamhas'* alias 'Thomas'. Examples date from the fifteenth century. Charles Tais settled in Georgia in 1768.

TAIT, TATE. Originally possibly either an Anglo-Saxon name or one derived from the Norse word *'teitr'* meaning 'cheerful'. The surname appears in Scottish records from the fourteenth century. David Tait was granted land in West Florida in 1769, and John Tate emigrated to Georgia in 1774.

TANNIS. A very unusual surname of unknown origin. Agnes Tannis was transported to East New Jersey in 1685.

TANNYHILL. Territorial, derived from a place in Ayrshire. An uncommon surname. Examples date from the sixteenth century. John and Robert Tanyhill, both farmers, emigrated to New York in 1774.

TARBET. Territorial, from Tarbet in Easter Ross, used as a surname since the fourteenth century. Derived from *'tairbeart'* meaning 'isthmus'. Hugh Tarbet was in Boston by 1756.

TASSIE. Possibly an occupational surname indicating a 'seller of bags and purses' derived from the French word *'tassie'*. Examples in Scotland date from the sixteenth century. William Tassie, a smith from Glasgow, emigrated to Salem in 1775.

TAYLOR. One of the most common surnames of occupational origin. Originally French *'tailleur'* meaning 'a cloth cutter' it has been recognised as a surname since the thirteenth century. Peter Taylor, a carpenter, emigrated to Cape Fear in 1750, and James Taylor, from Aberdeen, emigrated to Virginia in 1667.

TELFORD. A variant of 'Telfer'. A Norman French occupational surname meaning 'blacksmith'. A surname in Scotland since the thirteenth century. John Telford emigrated to Virginia in 1774.

TELLER. Possibly a Dutch surname. William Teller was transported to New England in 1651.

TEMPLE. Territorial, taken from the village of Temple in Midlothian, once the Scottish headquarters of the Knights Templar. William Temple was transported to the West Indies in 1678.

TEMPLETON. Territorial, based on the place-name in Ayrshire, with a possible link to the Knights Templar. Used as a surname since the thirteenth century Isobel Templeton, from Ayrshire, was transported to Virginia in 1772.

TENNANT. A surname derived from holding land by which a livelihood is earned. Examples of the surname date from the thirteenth century. James Tennant, a Covenanter, was transported to Carolina in 1684

TERRIS. Territorial, derived from Tarras in Morayshire. Varying examples of the surname are noted since the fourteenth century. Andrew Terris was transported to Boston in 1651.

TEVIOTDALE. Territorial originating in a place in Roxburghshire. Examples can be dated back to the thirteenth century. James Teviotdale, a horse thief, was banished to the American colonies in 1754.

THANE, THAIN. An occupational surname derived from the Old English word '*thegn*' meaning a 'soldier'. Examples date back to the twelfth century. Rev. Daniel Thain, from Aberdeen, died in New Jersey during 1763.

THOM. A diminutive of 'Thomas' or possibly a modified version of 'MacThom'. Examples date back to the fifteenth century. John Thom, from Glasgow, was transported to Maryland in 1704.

THOMSON, THOMPSON. One of the most common patronymical surnames in Scotland, signifying 'son of Thom'. Found in Scotland since the fourteenth century. John Thomson, from Argyll, was banished to New England in 1685, and Rev. Andrew Thomson died in Virginia in 1719.

THORBURN. A patronymic based on the Scandinavian personal name '*Thorbrand*'. A surname in Scotland since the fourteenth century. William Thorburn, a Jacobite, was transported to Antigua in 1747.

THORNTON. Territorial, originating in a place-name in Kincardineshire. Used as a surname since the early thirteenth century. James Thornton emigrated to New York in 1774

THREIPLAND. A territorial surname based on a place in Kilbucho, Peebles-shire. Examples date from the thirteenth century. and became localised in Perthshire by the seventeenth century. John Thripland was in Boston by 1721.

TILLERY. Territorial, a surname taken from a place-name in Aberdeenshire. Andrew Tillery, a Jacobite from Aberdeen, was transported to Maryland in 1747.

TODD, TOD. A descriptive surname likening someone to a 'tod' or 'fox'. Recorded in Scotland since the thirteenth century. Quentin Tod, a goat thief, was banished to Barbados in 1666, while William Tod, a coachbuilder from Edinburgh, settled in Philadelphia before 1775.

TODSHALL. A placename formed from 'tod' meaning 'fox', and 'hall' which probably is an Anglicisation of 'haugh' or 'meadow', thus 'the fox's meadow'. A very unusual surname. John Todshall was transported to Barbados in 1665.

TOLMIE. A Gaelic surname found in Inverness-shire and the Hebrides. Donald Tolmie emigrated from Stornaway to Philadelphia in 1775, Alexander Tolmie died in Georgia during 1736, and Alexander Tolmie, from Cork, emigrated to New York in 1774

TORRANCE. A territorial surname from places in Stirlingshire and in Lanarkshire of that name. Based on a Gaelic name *'torran'* meaning 'little hill'. Examples of the surname date from the sixteenth century. Torrance was a storekeeper in Falmouth, Virginia, before 1776

TORRIE. Based on a Gaelic word *'torr'* meaning a hill, it can have originated from a number of places, especially one in Aberdeen and another in Dumfries-shire. Examples date back to the medieval period. John Torry, from Paisley, emigrated via Pennsylvania to North Carolina around 1765.

TOSH. An abbreviation of 'Macintosh', see above. David Tosh, a pedlar and horsethief from Angus, was banished to America in 1767.

TOSHACH. A descriptive surname based on a Gaelic word *'toisech'* meaning 'leader'. Used as a surname since the thirteenth century. David Toshach, from Perthshire, settled in East New Jersey in 1684, and William Tosh died in Rhode Island in 1685..

TOUGH. Territorial, derived from the parish of Tough, Aberdeenshire. Based on a Gaelic word *'tulach'* meaning 'a knoll'. Used as a surname since the fourteenth century. Alistair Tough, a Cromwellian transportee, landed in Boston in 1652.

TOWARD. Territorial, derived from the lands of Toward in Argyllshire. Janet Toward was transported from Edinburgh to Maryland in 1704. Clan Lamont.

TOWER. Originally a French surname *'de Tour'*. Traditionally associated with Aberdeenshire. Dr James Tower, was educated at Marischal College, Aberdeen, around 1775, settled in St Thomas in the West Indies, and Patrick Tower was transported to New England in 1651.

TRAILL. A surname first noted in Fife during the fourteenth century, and later in Orkney and Caithness. Rev. William Trail, settled on the Potomac River in 1682, and William Traill, from Orkney, emigrated to Georgia in 1775.

TRAN, TRAYNE. A surname of unknown origin found in Cumberland in the fourteenth century and in Ayrshire by the fifteenth century. Hugh Tran, a Glasgow merchant, settled in St Kitts by 1768, and Alexander Tran was in Boston by 1735..

TRENT. Territorial, possibly a corruption of Tranent in East Lothian. Examples date from the fifteenth century. Lawrence Trent was a merchant in Barbados by 1689, and William Trent was in Boston during 1697.

TROOP, TROUP. Territorial, originating with the name of lands in Banffshire and used as a surname since the thirteenth century. Robert Troup died in Morris County, New York, in 1769, and John Troop emigrated to Prince Edward Island in 1775.

TROTTER. An occupational surname from *'trotteur'*, French meaning 'messenger'. A borders clan based in Berwickshire since the fourteenth century. Alexander Trotter was in Boston by 1716, and Richard Trotter was in the Virginia Regiment during 1756.

TULLIDEPH. Territorial, derived from lands of that name in Angus. A rare surname. Dr Walter Tullideph died in Antigua in 1772.

TULLOCH. A territorial surname originating in a place near Dingwall. In Gaelic *'tulach'* means 'hill' or 'mound'. A surname since the fourteenth century. Magnus Tilloch, from Orkney, was in Boston by 1749, and John Tulloch, from Orkney, settled in Georgia during 1775.

TUNNOCK, TUNNO. Possibly from the Gaelic personal name *'Tonnaigh'*. Thomas Tunno was in East Florida by 1786

TURNBULL, TRUMBELL. Probably from the Old English name 'Trumbald' meaning 'strongly bold'. A major Borders reiving clan since the medieval period. Dr Andrew Turnbull, from Annan, was prominent in the settlement of East Florida before the Revolution

TURNER. A surname of occupational origin from *'tornour'*, French meaning 'lathe worker'. Used as a surname since the fourteenth century. Charles Turner, and his sons Charles and John, all masons from Wigtown, emigrated to North America in 1774.

THE SCOTTISH SURNAMES OF COLONIAL AMERICA

TURPNEY. A rare surname possibly of Norse origin recorded in Scotland since the seventeenth century. John Turpney, a Covenanter, was transported to East New Jersey in 1685.

TWEED. A surname used to describe a place of residence – by the river Tweed. Alexander Tweed, from Banff, was a planter and merchant in Carolina before 1776.

TWEEDIE. Territorial, derived from the lands of Tweedie in Lanarkshire and used as a surname since the thirteenth century. Janet Tweedie, from Roxburghshire, was banished to the American colonies in 1764.

TYTLER. A rare surname of unknown origin. R. Tytler died in Boston during 1771.

URE. An abbreviation of MacUre, a variant of MacIver. An uncommon surname. Alexander ure, a weaver from Dunbartonshire, emigrated to South Carolina in 1684, and James Ure landed in Boston during 1768.

URIE. Territorial, originating in the lands of Urie near Stonehaven. Examples of the surname date from the thirteenth century. Five Covenanters bearing the surname Urie were banished to the American Plantations in the late seventeenth century.

URQUHART. Territorial, based on the old barony of Urquhart on Loch Ness –side. A surname since the fourteenth century. Rev. John Urquhart settled in Maryland in 1732, and Rev. William Urquhart was on Long Island, New York from 1702 to 1709.

VALENTINE. A Latin name found in north-east Scotland since the fourteenth century. Andrew Valentine emigrated to Quebec in 1775.

VALLANCE. A French surname introduced into Scotland by the Anglo-Normans during the twelfth century. Robert Vallance was transported from Glasgow to Maryland in 1728

VANS, VAUS, VASS, VOICE. A surname introduced into Scotland by the Anglo-Normans in the twelfth century. Charles Vass died in Darien during 1699, Jane Voice settled in South Carolina in 1767, and David Vance emigrated from Ireland to Nova Scotia by 1761.

VEITCH, VEACH. A surname introduced into Scotland by the Anglo-Normans in the twelfth century. William Veatch died in Darien during 1699, and Samuel Vetch, from Edinburgh, was Governor of Nova Scotia in 1710.

VELLZON. A rare territorial surname derived from a place on Harray, Orkney, and used as a surname since the sixteenth century. Andrew Vellzon, from Birsay, Orkney, was in Boston by 1750.

VERNOR. A surname of uncertain origin found in Scotland since the fifteenth century. James Vernor emigrated to East New Jersey in 1685

VILANT, VIOLENT. Possibly a Huguenot surname. David Violant, from Edinburgh, died in New York in 1710.

VINIAN. Possibly a variant of the Gaelic name *'Fionnan'* which appears as Finnan in Dumfries and Galloway since the seventeenth century. Henry Vinian from Ayrshire, was in Boston by 1766.

WADDELL. Territorial, taken from Wedale in Midlothian. Examples date back to the early thirteenth century. Thomas Waddell, from Prestonpans, died in Darien in 1699, and James Waddell was in Boston by 1737.

WAIT. An occupational surname derived from the Middle English word *'waite'* meaning 'watchman'. Examples in Scotland date from the early fourteenth century. Hugh Wait, a farmer from Neilston, emigrated to America in 1775.

WALES. Probably a variant of Wallace, (see below). Margaret Wales, from Dundee, emigrated to Maryland in 1684.

WALKER. An occupational surname *'waulker'* equivalent to 'fuller' – one who expands woollen cloth. A common surname in Scotland since the fourteenth century. Alexander Walker, a Jacobite from Bervie, was transported to Maryland in 1747, while James Walker, a blacksmith, emigrated to Philadelphia in 1774.

WALKINGSHAW. A territorial surname based on a placename in Renfrewshire and used as a surname since the sixteenth century. The name may come from *'Wealcere'* and *'sceaga'* meaning 'the fuller's wood'. John Walkingshaw was in Boston by 1685 and William Walkingshaw was there in 1731.

WALLACE. Probably based on the Old English word *'welisc'* meaning 'foreigner' a term used to describe the native Celtic people of Britain, including the Britons of Strathclyde. The surname is first found in Ayrshire and Renfrewshire during the twelfth century. David Wallace, from Stonehaven, settled in Virginia in 1723, and Margaret Wallace, from Edinburgh, was transported to Maryland in 1704.

WALLET. A surname of unknown origins found in Dumfries-shire. John Wallet, a Covenanter, was transported to America in 1685.

WALLS. Possibly a variant of 'Wallace' or alternatively a territorial surname from Walls in Orkney. Herbert Walls, a Covenanter from Dumfries-shire, was transported to America in 1684.

WALSTON. A territorial surname taken from a place of that name near Biggar in Lanarkshire, originally 'Wallacetown'.

WANLESS. A Northumbrian surname of unknown origin. Recorded in Scotland since the fifteenth century. Alexander Wanless, from Perth, was transported to the American colonies in 1758.

WARD. Derived from a Gaelic occupational name '*Bhaird*' meaning 'bard', or from the Old English name '*weard*' meaning 'watchman' or 'guard'. A surname recorded in Scotland since the fourteenth century and also in Ireland. Hugh and Miles Ward emigrated from Scotland to North Carolina in 1739.

WARDEN. Possibly an occupational surname but probably a territorial one derived from Warden in Northumberland. A surname once localised in Angus and Fife. Rev. James Warden emigrated to Virginia in 1711, settling in James City, while Ebenezer Warden, a wright and thief from Leith was transported to Maryland in 1771.

WARDLAW. A territorial surname derived from one of several places in Scotland. The name suggests 'a hill used to keep watch from'. A surname since the fourteenth century. Ralph Wardlaw was in Pensacola by 1766.

WARDROPE, WARDROBE, WODRUP. An occupational surname, derived from the office of keeper of the royal wardrobe. A surname in Scotland since the early thirteenth century. James Wardrope, a merchant, sailed to the West Indies in 1684, and Joseph Wardrope, a house carpenter from Edinburgh, settled in Georgia in 1733.

WARK. Territorial, taken from Wark in Northumberland. Examples date back to the fifteenth century. John Wark, a millwright, settled in Georgia in 1774, and Robert Wark, a housebreaker from Glasgow, was transported to the American colonies in 1772.

WARNOCK, WARNOCH. A diminutive of '*Macilvernock*' from the Gaelic '*Mac Gille Mhearnaig*' meaning 'son of the servant of Ernaig'. A surname found in west central Scotland since the fifteenth century. Robert Warnock was transported to the American Plantations in 1684.

WARREN, WARRAND. Territorial, derived from Varenne a town near Dieppe in France. A Norman- French surname introduced to Scotland during the thirteenth century. James Warrand, a farmer from Strathspey, emigrated to New York in 1774, and Thomas Warren, the Attorney General, died in Antigua in 1779.

WARRENDER. A surname of occupational origin, a warrender or warrener being the equivalent of a gamekeeper. An unusual surname dating from the thirteenth century. William Warrender died on the Darien Expedition of 1699.

WARWICK. An English territorial surname either from Warwick, Warwickshire, or Warwick, Cumberland, and recorded in Scotland since the thirteenth century. Anthony Warwick was a storekeeper in Virginia from 1761.

WATERSON. Patronymic meaning 'son of Walter', a surname since the early modern period mainly found in the Lothians. William Waterson emigrated to New York in 1774 and settled in Vermont.

WATSON. Patronymic, meaning 'son of Wat or Walter', a very common Scots surname which has been recorded since the fourteenth century. Peter Watson, from Kelso, settled in East New Jersey in 1685, and James Watson was a planter in Barbados by 1655.

WATT. Patronymic, a diminutive of 'Walter', found mainly in the north-east since the sixteenth century. James Watt, a merchant from Panbride, settled in Virginia by 1775, and Robert Watt, a merchant from Edinburgh, settled in New York by 1717.

WATTIE. Another diminutive of 'Walter'. John Wattie, was transported from Aberdeen to Virginia in 1760.

WAUCHOPE. Territorial, taken from Wauchopedale in Dumfries-shire. The meaning may be from the Old Norse for *'warm valley'*. A surname since the twelfth century. Elizabeth Wauchope, from Edinburgh, was transported to the American Plantations in 1695, and John Wachope died in South Carolina in 1739.

WAUGH. A surname from the Borders, possibly an abbreviation of the surname Wauchope, in use since the thirteenth century. Wellwood Waugh led a group of emigrants from Dumfries to Prince Edward Island in 1775 and settled in Pictou.

WEBSTER. Occupational, meaning 'weaver'. A surname since the medieval period in Scotland. James Webster, a Jacobite, was exiled to Maryland in 1716, and David Webster, a gunner, died in Virginia before 1767.

WEDDERBURN. Territorial, derived from the lands of Wedderburn in Berwickshire. An English term meaning 'stream of the sheep'. Used as a surname since the thirteenth century. James Wedderburn settled in Charleston, South Carolina, before 1734.

WEDDERSTON, WEATHERTON. Territorial, a place name signifying the '*sheep settlement*'. A surname recorded in the eastern Borders from the seventeenth century. John Wedderston, a surgeon from Galashiels, settled in Kingston, Jamaica, before 1773.

WEEK. A variant of 'Wake' a surname found in Dumfries-shire during the fourteenth century. Alexander Week emigrated to Virginia in 1774.

WEIR. A surname of Norman origin introduced into Scotland during the twelfth century. Mary Weir was transported to Virginia in 1670 and Robert Weir, a painter from Edinburgh, died in Jamaica 1761.

WELSH, WALSH. From the Old English word '*walh*' meaning foreigner and used by them to describe the native British. Archibald Welsh was transported to the American colonies in 1751.

WEMYSS, WEEMS. Territorial, derived from Wemyss in Fife, and used as a surname since the thirteenth century. Wemyss comes from the Gaelic '*uaim*' meaning 'cave'. Alexander Wemyss died in New York in 1782, and James Wemyss was in Boston by 1695.

WEST. A surname recorded in Scotland since the seventeenth century. James West, from Aberdeen, was in Boston by 1765.

WHAIR. A variation of Weir found in Caithness. William Whair, from Wick, settled in Richmond County, Georgia, in 1775.

WHARRY. An abbreviation of *MacWharry*' or '*MacQuarrie*', Gaelic, meaning 'son of Guaire'. Most early examples come from sixteenth century Lanarkshire. James Wharry, a Covenanter, was transported to the American Plantations in 1681.

WHITE, WHYTE. Based on an Old English personal name and used as a surname in Scotland since the eleventh century. Rev. James White settled in Kingston, Jamaica, before 1692 and James White, a Covenanter, was transported to New York in 1684.

WHITEBURN. A territorial surname, taken from Whitburn in West Lothian. Used as a surname since the thirteenth century.

WHITEFORD, WHITEFOORD. Territorial, based on the lands of Whitefoord near Paisley. Used as a surname since the thirteenth century. James Whiteford settled in Maryland in 1730.

WHITEHEAD. A descriptive surname found in Scotland since 1300. James Whitehead, a cordiner from Edinburgh, settled in Virginia in 1773..

WHITELAW. Territorial, from the barony of Whitelaw in Roxburghshire. Examples date from the thirteenth century. Elizabeth Whitelaw, a Covenanter, was banished to East New Jersey in 1685, and Elspeth Whitelaw was transported to Barbados in 1663.

WHITING. Originally and Anglo-Saxon forename *'Hwiting'* meaning 'son of Hwita'. Many of the early examples come from Edinburgh and date from the fourteenth century. James Whiting was in Boston by 1705 and Andrew Whiting was there in 1731.

WIDROW, WOODROW. Occupational, derived from the post of 'wood-reeve' or forest manager. Jean Widrow emigrated from Islay to New York in 1740

WILDRIGE. An Orcadian surname. James Wildrige emigrated to Georgia in 1774.

WILKIE. Patronymic, another diminutive of 'William'. used as a surname in Scotland since the fourteenth century. James Wilkie, a Jacobite, was transported to South Carolina in 1716, and Isobel Wilkie emigrated to Dominica in 1773.

WILKINSON. Patronymic, signifying *'son of little William'*. Examples in Scotland date from the fifteenth century. Alexander Wilkinson settled in South Carolina in 1785.

WILL. Patronymic – as a diminutive of 'William'. Used as a surname in Scotland since the fifteenth century. Lauchlan Will, from Aberdeenshire, was transported to Virginia in 1773.

WILLIAMSON. Patronymic, signifying 'son of William'. A common surname in Scotland since the fourteenth century. Andrew Williamson, from Shetland, emigrated to North Carolina in 1775, while Peter Williamson, who was kidnapped and sold as a servant in Pennsylvania, returned to Scotland to successfully sue his kidnappers.

WILLIS. A patronymic meaning 'Willy's son', a surname dating from the thirteenth century. James Willis, from Shetland, was in Boston by 1733.

THE SCOTTISH SURNAMES OF COLONIAL AMERICA

WILLOCKS, WILLOX. Probably a variation of the English surname *'Willcock'* meaning 'little William'. Found in north east Scotland since the sixteenth century. Alexander Willox, a surveyor from Morayshire, died in Jamaica during 1760.

WILSON. One of the most common of Scottish surnames. A patronymic meaning 'son of Will', used since the medieval period. Also common in Ulster. William Wilson, a Covenanter, was banished to East New Jersey in 1685, while Robert Wilson, an apothecary and surgeon from Fife, emigrated to South Carolina in 1753, and Thomas Wilson emigrated from Larne to Charleston in 1772.

WINDWICK. A surname of territorial origin derived from Windwick on Ronaldsay one of the Orkney Islands. Virtually all early examples come from that island. The suffix *'wick'* is from the Norse word *'vik'* indicating a bay. Janet Windwick, from Grimness, South Ronaldsay, was banished to the American colonies in 1769.

WINGATE. A surname of territorial origin derived from Wingate in Northumberland. Examples in Scotland date from the sixteenth century. Rev. John Wingate settled in Dale, Virginia, in 1771.

WINTER. Derived from an Old English personal name. Used as a surname in Scotland since the twelfth century. Edward Winter from Edinburgh, was transported to Barbados in 1685.

WISE. Probably a descriptive surname. Examples date from the fourteenth century. Ninian Wise, a Jacobite, was transported to Maryland in 1747.

WISHART. Derived from an Old French word *'wischard'* meaning wise. Recorded in Scotland since around 1200. William Wishart was transported to Carolina in 1684, and Elizabeth Wishart settled in New York by 1777.

WITHERSPOON, WOTHERSPOON, WEATHERSPOON. This is a surname of uncertain origin although the first element *'wither'* may come from the Old English word for a 'lamb'. Examples date from the thirteenth century. Reverend John Witherspoon, from East Lothian, signed the Declaration of Independence in 1776, and Robert Witherspoon was in Boston by 1713.

WOOD. Probably a locational surname indicating a place of residence. Examples date back to the thirteenth century. Reverend Alexander Wood went to Carolina in 1707, and David Wood, a Jacobite, was transported to Maryland in 1747.

WOODHALL. A territorial surname taken from one of two places in Scotland. John Woodall was transported to New England in 1651.

WRIGHT. A surname of occupational origin, the Scottish equivalent of the English 'carpenter'. Recorded as early as the thirteenth century. John Wright, a Covenanter, was banished to Virginia in 1668, while William Wright, a Jacobite, was exiled to Virginia in 1716.

WYLLIE. A diminutive of 'William' used as a surname since the fourteenth century. Also found in Ulster. Reverend William Wyllie settled in Albemarle, Virginia, before 1740, and Thomas Wyllie, a weaver, emigrated to Philadelphia in 1774.

YATES, YEATS. A descriptive term indicating a place of residence 'near the gate', *'yet'* being an old word for 'gate'. Examples date from the fourteenth century. Francis Yates, a Jacobite, was transported to Maryland in 1747, and Benjamin Yeats emigrated to Virginia in 1720.

YEAMAN. From the Middle English word indicating a rural dweller. Examples of the surname in Scotland date from the sixteenth century. James Yeaman, a Dundee barber, emigrated to Philadelphia in 1775.

YORSTON. A territorial surname derived from lands in Corstorphine near Edinburgh. A surname largely localised near Edinburgh and in Orkney, examples date from the fifteenth century. Janet Yorstoun was transported to New York in 1715.

YOUNG. A descriptive surname used in Scotland since the medieval period. Andrew Young, from Stirling, emigrated to New York in 1775, and Robert Young, a Covenanter, was transported to East New Jersey in 1685.

YOUNGER. A surname of Flemish origin derived from *'Joncker'*. Recorded in Scotland since the fourteenth century. John Younger was transported from Leith to Barbados in 1653, and William Younger was transported from Leith to the American Plantations in 1679.

YOUNGHUSBAND. A very rare surname in Scotland. John Younghusband emigrated via Inverness to Georgia in 1737.

YULE, YUILL, YOOL. A surname of unknown origin which has been recorded in Scotland since the fourteenth century. John Yuille, a merchant from Dunbartonshire, died in Williamsburg, Virginia, in

1746, while Elspeth Yuill was transported from Edinburgh to Barbados in 1663.

www.ingramcontent.com/pod-product-compliance
Lightning Source LLC
Chambersburg PA
CBHW050528270326
41926CB00015B/3118